THE CALM TECHNIQUE

The Calm Technique

PAUL WILSON

Thorsons
An Imprint of HarperCollins*Publishers*

Thorsons
An Imprint of HarperCollins*Publishers*
77–85 Fulham Palace Road,
Hammersmith, London W6 8JB

First published by Thorsons 1987
Second edition 1995
This edition 1997
Originally published by Greenhouse Publications Pty Ltd,
385 Bridge Road, Richmond, Victoria, Australia, 1985
   5 7 9 10 8 6 4

© The Calm Centre Pty Ltd

Paul Wilson asserts the moral right to
be identified as the author of this work

A catalogue record for this book
is available from the British Library

ISBN 0 7225 3626 7

Printed and bound in Great Britain by
Woolnough Bookbinding Limited, Irthlington, Northamptonshire

Contents

Introduction

'Close your eyes and you will see clearly,
Cease to listen and you will hear truth.'

IF WE'RE HONEST WITH OURSELVES, we'll
almost certainly see room for improvement in our lives.
We can be more contented. We can be healthier,
happier and more peaceful. We can eliminate many of
the life-shortening risks that surround us.

It is a well-publicized fact that one's health,
happiness and harmony can be dramatically enhanced
by concentrating on four lifestyle areas:

1) Diet
2) Exercise
3) Attitude
4) Meditation

But can you achieve significant results by following just one of these routes?

The answer is yes. A rigorous devotion to exercise will have a marked effect on the overall quality of your life. So will a similar devotion to diet or attitude. The deal is obviously a balanced pursuit of all four areas: then the effects of one will compliment the other, and the effectiveness of each is enhanced by the practice of the other.

If your determination is such that you can pursue all four categories with equal effort and sincerity, your energies will be rewarded manyfold. However, the one which has the greatest single capacity for life improvement and fulfilment is meditation. Even though this book stresses the importance of all four areas and contains chapters on each, it is mainly concerned with meditation.

The traditional approach to a book on this subject is from the mystical point of view. When you consider that most publications have been written by mystics of one sort or another, and that many of the teachings have been the products of various mystical schools, this is understandable.

What will distinguish this book from the others is my intention to describe the wonders of meditation without the magic and the mysticism. In writing, I have endeavoured to explain everything in everyday language, to avoid exaggeration, and to keep in check my enthusiasm for this subject. You may be familiar with the religious writer's favourite literary devices, mystical metaphors, parables and allegories. While these may be much lauded techniques in traditional writing, they can often be elaborate and exotic ways of saying very little and, as such, have no place in this book. Nevertheless, as much of the material here concerns the most intimate workings of the human mind and psyche, the use of the metaphor will be a necessary convention from time to time. Care must be taken so that metaphor does not become confused with fact. A phrase like 'the body becomes light' is nothing more than an attempt to convey a subtle feeling; you should not run to the bathroom scales in anticipation of a Weight Watchers miracle. There are no miracles to be had.

Unfortunately, meditation will always be shrouded in mysticism (as it has been), that is the nature of the art. While I feel no compulsion to try to alter this state of affairs, I do feel obliged not to add it. Hence this book (and the Calm Technique itself) does tend to err on the side of the practical rather than the romantic. It was written in the belief that meditation is a useful, easy-to-understand exercise that deserves to be treated as matter-of-factly as aerobics or diet.

Those of you who have ever tried to learn about meditation from some of the traditional sources will probably know the frustration that goes hand in hand with this search. If you were reluctant to subscribe to a new set of beliefs, or to pay dearly for a course in mystical studies, you didn't have many choices. I am not for one moment questioning the sincerity and credibility of these teachers of meditation, I know and trust many, and their teachings come from a much longer lineage than mine. However, the Calm Technique presents many of their teachings in a much simplified way and sacrifices very little in order to do so. Still, should you ever want to continue your studies beyond the scope of this book, you will find the Calm Technique an excellent starting point.

I must also emphasize at the outset that this book is concerned mainly with the temporal aspect of meditation: the emotional and physical benefits. I have no guru aspirations or pretensions, and have never been blessed with more than my fair share of cosmic revelation or understanding. Nor do I have any better answers than the next person as to the True Meaning of Life. All I have to offer is an exhaustively researched synthesis of a considerable number of relaxation and meditation techniques which really works. I will show you how to get more out of life, overcome many of the pains and pressures of modern existence and develop a better understanding of what your life is about.

In many respects, the Calm Technique isn't anything terribly new. I've borrowed shamelessly (we call it 'research') from well-worn ascetic practices and schools of meditation. As a result, the Calm Technique exhibits many of the time-proven principles and methods which have been in use for the past 5000 years. Students of some other schools of meditation may recognize this as being somewhat similar to their own. One would hope that they would find the Calm Technique considerably easier to understand and apply.

There are hundreds of religions, sects and common-interest groups in the world today whose objectives are similar to those expressed in this book. But the Calm Technique has no involvement or affiliation whatsoever with any of these groups. Nor does it require you to have any specific spiritual attitudes or beliefs, or to subscribe to any particular philosophy or moral code. Apart from putting aside a little time each day (just as you would for any exercise programme), it doesn't require you to alter your lifestyle in any way at all.

The objective which all people who read this book will almost certainly share is an improvement in the quality of life. A healthier, happier, more meaning-ful life is a goal we all seek, but which few of us search for with any great determination. How often do we vow to follow some course of action which will improve our health or attitude, only to find that the novelty soon wears off and we abandon it in favour of another message, a newer fad, or worse still, nothing at all?

Before you go any further, it is worth reflecting on what you really expect to find from a publication such as this. Are you seeking some new experience? Do you have a strong desire to improve the quality of your life, the way you feel, the way you think, the way you relate to the rest of the world? Perhaps it's just curiosity. Would you like to be a more relaxed, peaceful and contented person? Are you waiting for someone to offer you a new direction? An answer? An easy way out? Are you approaching this subject with an open mind, or do you already have preconceived ideas on what it is about?

It is important for you to identify your needs and expectations right from the beginning. Only by knowing what you want can you hope to achieve it through the Calm Technique. That may sound elementary, but it is a vital consideration when dealing with such a subtle experience.

The Calm Technique is a very simple, easy-to-learn exercise which will produce substantial and positive results for anyone who tries it. Nevertheless, the biggest obstacle you will face in using it successfully is your own expectation. If you start out with a fixed idea of how it's all meant to work, you stand a very good chance of being confused or disappointed. Disregard all those things you've heard and read, approach the subject with a completely open mind, and you won't be disappointed. Forget all those popular misconceptions that promise exotic experiences which range from 'nothingness' to Nirvana. Forget about those stories of mystical rapture. This book contains no miracles, no occultism, and no promise of immediate enlightenment. Nor is it a source of cheap thrills or cosmic experiences.

I suspect it's a very important marketing technique for a 'how to' book to guarantee instant and permanent results with only a minimum of application and effort. I hope you won't be too disappointed to learn that such successes are seldom forthcoming in real life. Despite how fervently we wish it were true, there are no shortcuts and no easy ways out when it comes to achieving the goals in life that we consider important. If you want a happier, healthier, more harmonious existence, you have to work for it. You have to make the effort. You have to spend the time. But with an open mind, a sincere desire to succeed and the Calm Technique, these goals are easily attained and can have the most profound and positive effects on your life.

The Calm Technique is so simple and easy to remember that you could easily learn it in two minutes. Then how come you've got to read a whole book? First, because it is important that you clearly understand what the experience is going to be like, *before* you begin. Second, you have to know what you can expect to gain from using the Calm Technique. And finally, there is the ever-present risk that any sort of aberrant techniques learned in the early stages will be difficult to 'unlearn'. Therefore, it is imperative that you approach it from the beginning … so you'll have to read the whole book.

This book should take you only two or three hours to read. *For the best results, read it in a quiet and peaceful place – away from people, traffic fumes and television sets. A calm setting will dramatically increase the effectiveness of the reading.*

I doubt if there has been a 'how to' book yet written which omits a paragraph about patience, about waiting until you've read it all before you try a thing. I'm afraid I've broken no new ground with *The Calm Technique*. It also asks you to refrain from experimenting (except where instructions say otherwise) until you've finished the entire book.

The Calm Technique has so much to offer. It will work for you. You will see the benefits. You will find it easy to learn. I'm so eager to tell you about it that I can hardly wait for you to turn the page!

SECTION I

CHAPTER I

The Calm Technique

'To see a world in a grain of sand
And a Heaven in a wild flower,
Hold infinity in the palm of your hand
And eternity in an hour.'
William Blake

THIS IS A BOOK ON MEDITATION.
For many people today, the mere mention of the
word 'meditation' is enough to have them reaching
for the phone book in search of deprogrammers while
muttering things about secret cults, sleep deprivation
and protein deficiencies. It conjures up all sorts of
exotic images of saffron robes, incense, chants, prayer
and Eastern gobbledegook. Indeed, much of the
research for this book has been conducted within these

latter environments (although I have yet to encounter a genuine 'secret cult').

In spite of overwhelming evidence to the contrary, the misapprehension persists that meditation is inextricably linked with religious knowledge and understanding. I'm sure this attitude continues as much because of the romantic notions and enlistment techniques of the organizations that teach it, as it does from any intrinsic characteristic of meditation itself. Faith, rituals and philosophies are not essential for effective meditation. The physical and emotional rewards alone, while not necessarily the ultimate expressions of all that is possible within the art, are reasons enough for practising it.

The Calm Technique is mainly concerned with the temporal aspects of meditation: the physical and emotional benefits. Its primary intention is to improve your quality of life, your health and your understanding. This is achieved through a physiological state we call the Calm State, which is one of great peace and calm.

When you achieve this state, stress-related problems will begin to diminish or vanish completely. You will begin to develop a sense of wellbeing and confidence like you haven't felt in a long, long time. You will sleep better, eat better, think better, live better. In short, you'll feel great to be alive.

Obviously, for those who are so inclined, meditation can bring profound spiritual rewards as well. Those of you who are mainly concerned with spiritual enlightenment should consider the Calm Technique as the first step on a long, hard road. For such a search, this book is only a beginning. The Calm Technique can help you free your consciousness to pursue higher goals. When you have mastered it, you can combine the Calm Technique with prayer, readings from the various scriptures, as well as any of the other spiritual directions that are open to you. You should consider this as a major step in the right direction.

WHAT EXACTLY IS 'MEDITATION'?

Ask a thousand meditators to define 'meditation' in terms of their own experience, and you'll get a thousand different answers. This seems hardly surprising when you consider how personal and subjective the experience that takes place entirely within your mind is. What meditation does for one person may have little in common with what it does for another. As expectations and appreciations vary dramatically from one person to the next, it becomes clear why so many of the traditional schools resort to mysticism and vagueness.

But how can we define 'meditation'?

A really smug definition of meditation one regularly hears is: 'the best definition of meditation is the act of meditation itself'. Obviously, this is not a definition. However it is forgivable because, in many ways, 'meditation' is as much an abstraction as 'love' or 'envy', both of which are extremely difficult to define in experiential terms.

The really cosmic definition of meditation says it is the means of elevating the consciousness from the Lower Mind to the Higher Mind. The analogy which explains this phenomenon usually goes something like this: 'The Lower Mind equates with what you see around you now – daylight, trees, cars, dirty washing, highway hoardings. The Higher Mind equates with the changes in your perceptions if you were to take on a satellite point of view. You would see yourself as more a part of the Universe; your everyday surroundings would seem less important and less threatening; the higher you went, the more your horizons would be expanded.' While that is accurate to a certain extent, it is too heavenly and grandiose an explanation for someone just beginning meditation.

I believe meditation is best explained (if not defined) in a word: 'being'. When you learn how to live only in the moment; when nothing distracts you; when you are not tied to the past or anxious about the future; when your mind and your

emotions are your servants rather than your master, your consciousness (your awareness) is in the most perfect state possible. This state is simply 'being'. Meditation is about 'being'; not about 'doing'.

In meditation, you become peacefully aware of your real self: what you are and what your purpose is in life. The more you use it, the more aware you become. There is no flash of inspiration and enlightenment that allows you to shout: 'So that's what I really am!'; the experience is subtle and cumulative. By becoming aware of your real self (as opposed to the 'self' you like to present to the world, and indeed, the 'self' you may even pretend to yourself) you will no longer be a victim of the pressures and anxieties of modern life. When you learn to live for each moment, to enjoy and appreciate life to the fullest at that moment, you suddenly become impervious to the myriad of doubts and fears that you've lived with all your life. When you can finally appreciate that just 'being' is everything, that you cannot make life perform exactly as you would like it to, that you cannot control the future, and that there is no point in dwelling on what has passed, you will have achieved something that most people never come close to in a lifetime: you will have peace.

Meditation is subtle and habitual. It is not a one-off adventure or experience that will transport you into other worlds of cosmic ecstasy (well, not as far as I know). But there will almost surely be moments when you become blissfully unaware of the passage of time and the distractions of your own mind. There may even be times when you will be totally unaware of your very physical presence, yet be remarkably aware of your existence. Those are moments when you are just 'being', and they are moments to be treasured. When the mind is calmed, and external distractions and influences are eliminated, you will come in contact with the very essence of your understanding (being) and truly understand the meaning of peace.

WHY IT'S CALLED THE CALM TECHNIQUE

If I could give you just one thing that would greatly influence your life for the better, it would be a sense of Calm. Then, when the newspapers preach doom and gloom, the cost of living goes through the roof, your livelihood is threatened by computers and industrial robots, when the entire world is overwhelmed by feelings of impotence and despair, you will be confident, contented and living life to the fullest. You will enjoy a zest and enthusiasm for living that 'normal' people seldom feel. You will look forward to each day with a long-forgotten feeling of youthful adventure.

Quite a bonus for having a sense of Calm, wouldn't you say?

The Calm Technique is dedicated to developing this sense of Calm. Calm is what you experience while you're practising it (the Calm State), Calm is what you practise, and Calm is what you achieve as a result. This simple state, which is so easy to achieve, can have the most profound effect on your entire life.

The Calm Technique is a simple and straight-forward meditation technique which, with perseverance, can dramatically improve the way you think, the way you feel and the way you live. Simply by following the information contained within these pages, you will soon begin to experience its full potential and enjoy many of the benefits that the traditional avenues of meditation study have promised throughout the ages.

Simplicity is the key to the Calm Technique. Each step of the process is clearly set out in simple, easy-to-follow stages. This does not limit its effectiveness one bit. In fact, students of the Calm Technique who have learned other techniques tend to agree that the simplicity of the Calm Technique not only makes the process easier to appreciate, but actually enhances it.

I've said it before, and will say it many more times by the end of this book: the great advantage of the Calm Technique is that it really works! You will find it easy to understand and apply, you will begin to see positive results from the very first time you use it, and the benefits will become more and more obvious as you continue to practise it.

CHAPTER 2

The Problem of Stress

'For the man who has conquered his mind, it is his greatest friend; but for the man who fails to do so, his mind will be his greatest enemy.'
Sri Krsna

WHAT WAS THE BIG THREAT facing us in the papers this morning? Do you think the greenhouse effect is more threatening than the spread of AIDS? Do you think the growing number of homeless people is a greater worry than the growing number of long-term unemployed? Add to all this the personal pressures that influence our lives: pressures from family, relationships and employment; the ambitions and standards we set for ourselves; our health and wealth; all the doubts, fears and insecurities of our everyday lives … is it any wonder we're feeling tense?

If there was ever a period in history when we could hardly avoid falling victim to the ravages of stress and tension, it's now. Stress today is a big threat and claims just as many casualties (if not more) as the Plague did in the seventeenth century. And just as it took a major lifestyle adjustment to combat the Plague, a similar adjustment is needed today to combat stress.

Stress is popularly accepted as the most common promoter of disease and discomfort in the Western world. It is blamed for the escalating incidence of heart disease and the rising national blood pressure; it encourages almost every fashionable ailment from migraine to cancer; it reduces resistance to disease; it contributes to the rampant insanity and social disorders that confront us every day of our lives. It leads to hypertension, indigestion, constipation, palpitations, insomnia and impotence. It has been blamed for high blood pressure, the hardening of the arteries, strokes and suicide. Overall, it's encouraged more serious illness and suffering than any other known condition, yet it doesn't sound anywhere as frightening or ugly as cancer or leprosy or even, dare I say it, herpes. Such is the insidious nature of stress.

Unlike most ailments, stress doesn't pass with time. It is self-perpetuating. It builds and builds until it is a major influence on your mind and body, until it dominates almost every action you take, every emotion you feel, and every thought you think. Contrary to popular opinion, the reason for this is biological rather than neurotic. Humans, like all animals, are biologically equipped for regular episodes of 'fight or flight'. When confronted by a hostile animal or adversary, primitive men had the choice: either stay and fight, or flee for their lives. While deciding, their bodies were preparing for either eventuality. With no conscious effort, the adrenal glands began secreting adrenaline and epineph-rine hormones, muscles tensed, pulses quickened, blood pressure rose, digestion ceased, breathing quickened. They were perfectly equipped for either fight or flight.

In today's world, every mishap, confrontation, mistake, and almost every move we make seems to activate this 'fight or flight' mechanism. The early morning alarm fails to sound. You don't have a clean shirt. The garbage hasn't been collected again. The train runs late. The ticket collector is aggressive. You're late for work. Your best friend is angry because of something you said. You don't know how you're going to finish all your work this week. You discover you're the centre of a spicy piece of office gossip. And it's still only 9.20 a.m.

Each one of those 'unimportant' little aggravations activates the 'fight or flight' response in your body. You experience this physiological preparation for action hundreds of times throughout an average day. However, there are differences between your 'fight or flight' reaction and the primitive men's. They could resolve their stressful situations simply by performing one of the two options at their disposal: fighting or fleeing. Either way, the strain on their muscles used up the chemicals in their system, and they immediately began to calm down and their stress levels dissolved. In your case it's not so easy. When your 'fight or flight' mechanism is activated, you have to stay at your desk. Or behind the wheel of your cab. Or behind the sales counter. And all you can do is *brood*. Your nerves and muscles are all primed for fight or flight, your juices are flowing and there's nothing you can do about it. You're stuck in that passive situation while your stress level builds and builds.

Is it any wonder that your stress ends up at such critical levels?

This book is dedicated to eliminating stress.

I'm sure everyone recognizes the fact that it is possible to live a stress-free life. Yet, if you're like most people I know, you won't be prepared to make the dramatic lifestyle adjustment that's required to achieve this end. Like me, you're probably not prepared to change your occupation or husband, or move to a remote part of the country. Similarly, you're probably not prepared to reduce your diet to a subsistence level, to forget just how good wine tastes, to exercise at least thirty minutes a day, to concentrate only on positive thoughts, to get at least eight hours' sleep every night and to drink five litres of fluoride-free water every day.

There has to be a more practical solution than this!

There is. It is possible to live a progressively stress-free existence without making dramatic changes to your lifestyle. It is possible to face every day feeling calm and relaxed, easily coping with the pressures and anxieties that modern life presents. It is possible to enjoy a peaceful, happy, contented and confident existence, living life to the fullest. All with a minimum of guidance, surprisingly little effort, and the Calm Technique.

Primarily, the Calm Technique influences your state of mind. If your mind is calm, your life will be in order. As well, your state of mind has a very definite influence on your general state of health. Consider how a relaxed, happy, easy-going person always seems to have fewer medical complaints than someone who is neurotic, bitter and anxious. You may argue that the medical complaints could be the cause of the state of mind rather than the other way around; but evidence has shown that the mental state (read 'stress') does have a marked negative effect on organic conditions. Not only does it encourage ill-health and disease, but it inhibits the body's immune responses and the entire healing process.

Meditation not only encourages a powerful health-giving frame of mind, but it is also one of the most successful antidotes to stress. The Calm Technique *will* reduce accumulated stress. It will have a positive effect on your general state of mind and health. Use it sincerely and conscientiously, and the day will certainly come when you will no longer be a victim of stress.

CHAPTER 3

The Benefits

'One who overcomes others has force;
One who overcomes himself is strong.'
Taoist poem

WHAT MEDITATION WILL DO FOR YOU

THE BENEFITS OF MEDITATION are widely
documented and accepted today. Although it may be
considered to be the province of ageing hippies and New
Age types in some quarters, it is increasingly being used
as a creative and therapeutic exercise by people in all
walks of life.

The best thing I can say about the Calm Technique
is that you'll feel better after twenty minutes of
successful meditation than you will after twelve hours of

sleep. It is not intended to replace sleep, but it will leave you feeling more rested, more relaxed, and more alert.

The rewards that the Calm Technique will bring your way are many. As you read through its list of benefits, the claims of this programme may appear almost miraculous. This is not the case. You will not be overwhelmed by great physical and emotional transformation. The process is slow, subtle, cumulative and long term.

Think of it as an exercise programme. You begin in the knowledge that exercise is good for you. You know that twenty minutes one day per month is not enough, and that if you are to experience the full benefits of your efforts you must exercise regularly. So you do it regularly.

After your first couple of days, you will really feel like you have accomplished something. You're relaxed, you eat well, you sleep well. And as you work on it day by day, you become fitter and fitter.

Two months pass. You begin to think you're at your physical best (though common sense tells you there's still a long way to go). Now the day-to-day improvements aren't quite as noticeable. The novelty begins to wane. The importance seems to diminish. This is the period when most determination is needed. This is the turning point, where you either go on to become fit, or go back to where you started. The temptation to take it easy for a while gnaws at you – you don't need exercise, you're fit, this is all a waste of time. You have a choice: continue or take a 'harmless' break. If you abandon your exercise programme at this stage, you will soon become aware of how much good it was doing you; but by then it's too late and you have to start all over again. If, on the other hand, you had persevered during this slow period, you would be so much closer to your ultimate goal – fitness.

The Calm Technique works just like that. It's an exercise programme for the mind and emotions, if you like. As with the physical exercise programme, there is an immediate result. Then there is the tendency for you to become either impatient or blasé. If you persist, knowing that in the long term it will be well worth the effort, you will begin to notice significant improvements. You'll be more relaxed, more able to cope with everyday problems and annoyances, you'll have a greater capacity to enjoy life. Your wits will be keener and you'll be more creative. You'll have more energy, better health and a deeper (and ever-increasing) understanding of yourself, your life and how you relate to the world. In effect, you will flourish as a human being.

THE PHYSIOLOGICAL PROCESS

Since the West first began to take a serious interest in Yogic meditation at the turn of this century, there have been several notable studies of the physiological processes that take place during meditation. The most extensive and well reported studies took place primarily during the late 1960s at various US medical schools from Harvard to UCLA. There are enough books available on this subject for you to study it in as much detail as you can stand. For the purposes of this book, we will concern ourselves with a broad overview of these findings.

Meditation produces a state of deep relaxation (the Calm State) where, quite unlike sleep or hypnosis, your mind is wide awake and alert. During this state, some extraordinary things happen in your physiology.

There is a dramatic change in the pattern of your brainwaves. There is an increase in slow alpha waves, which are usually only present when you are wide awake and relaxed. Often there is an increase in theta waves, which relate to higher forms of consciousness such as creativity.

At the same time, as these alpha waves are evident, there is a definite presence of delta waves, which occur only in the deepest sleep. Brainwave patterns during meditation indicate a state of mind that is alert, creative, but in deep relaxation. By all conventional physiological standards, this is impossible. To compound the mystery even further, there is virtually no rapid eye movement

(REM) – an indication of sleep and dreaming – recorded in the meditative state.

Your metabolism is also affected (that's why you should avoid meditating directly after meals). Your oxygen consumption decreases about 20 per cent and you produce significantly less carbon monoxide. (Even in the deepest sleep, your decrease in oxygen consumption fails to equal those figures.) Your heartbeat and respiration rate decrease almost as dramatically. The lactate level in your bloodstream decreases by up to 50 per cent, nearly four times faster than in a state of deep relaxation! (Lactic acids are producing during the 'fight or flight' syndrome and contribute to feelings of anxiety, tension and fatigue.) Your blood pressure drops, and there is a definite increase in the electrical resistance of your skin (tension and anxiety induce a decrease in electrical resistance).

These remarkable physiological phenomena are unique to the meditative state and contribute to the great sense of peace, harmony and wellbeing you experience during the Calm Technique. Furthermore, these characteristics are the *opposite* to those you would find in a state of anxiety or anger. The Calm Technique produces an *opposite* response to that 'fight or flight' condition, and is therefore the most effective counter to stress and tension you can employ.

If you use the following checklist of life improvements after the first couple of weeks of the Calm Technique to test its effectiveness, you're having yourself on. While you will be aware of *some* benefits from the very beginning, others will develop with time and perseverance.

EMOTIONAL AND PSYCHOLOGICAL
IMPROVEMENTS ASSOCIATED WITH THE CALM
TECHNIQUE

You will be more positive.
You will be more alive, healthier, happier.
You will have a greater capacity to cope.
You will have an increase in mental alertness, and

will think and act more creatively.
You will eat better, sleep better, love better.
You will be more tolerant.
You will appreciate life more.

HOW CAN A 'SIMPLE EXERCISE' DO ALL THIS?

I'm asking you to believe a lot, aren't I? To believe that one very simple mental technique can bring all these wonderful benefits into your life. But it's true, and as you become more familiar with the practice you will begin to appreciate that everything in this book is easily attainable.

In the past few pages we have discussed the physiological changes that take place during the Calm Technique. During that twenty minutes of passive meditation, your physiological state becomes the *opposite* to that which exists when you're experiencing feelings of anxiety and tension. Your metabolic rate changes, your blood lactate level drops, even your skin produces an increase in electrical resistance. During the Calm Technique, you actually *reverse* the stress process! No doubt these phenomena are a direct result of your calm state of mind at the time, rather than any divine intervention or mystical process. This state of mind – the Calm State – is one of deep relaxation combined with extreme mental alertness, one which can only be attained through meditation.

Earlier we looked at other less tangible results of the Calm Technique, the emotional and spiritual advantages. Obviously, results in these areas can never be quantified to any acceptable scientific standard. No panel of scientists, no number of electrodes can ever prove to us exactly what emotional or attitudinal changes or improvements take place in the innermost recesses of a meditator's mind. These changes can only ever be vouched for by those who experience the benefits; that is, those who practise meditation. Unfortunately, you have no choice but to accept or reject their word on the subject. Consider though, that the popularity and credibility of meditation over such a long period of history has been maintained only through the testimony of its practitioners. Scientific evaluations of the physiological changes that take place have only been made in the past few decades.

But how do all these changes happen? What inspires them?

The one thing that almost all meditation techniques and practices have in common is single-mindedness, where the objective is to centre your attention on doing just one thing at one time with all your effort. So while there are many kinds of meditation – structured and unstructured, active and passive – they all share this same objective of doing one thing at a time.

When you have learned how to do one thing (and only one thing) at one time, you will have learned to centre your whole attention, to 'focus'. The Calm Technique will teach you to focus. This unique talent not only produces a wonderfully calm, balanced state of mind, but it also assists you in *all* aspects of your everyday life. You'll be able to think better, concentrate better, understand better. Your mind will be more creative. You'll function better in every respect.

One can only speculate how 'focusing' can bring about such positive results. It would seem that the act of doing just one thing frees the mind from unnecessary conflict and distraction to such an extent that mind and body function more perfectly than at any other time. Eastern mystics have claimed for centuries that this is your natural state, this is how you're really meant to feel and function *all the time*!

Think how your mind works when you're anxious. Your thoughts seem to come faster and faster. They flit from pillar to post every few seconds. They look sadly on the past and worry about the future. The more you try to slow them down, the more frantic they seem to become. Then, as your attention ebbs and flows in a hundred different directions, your anxiety level increases … one feeds the other until it's crisis time. 'I've really got to finish this work before the end of the day … where did I leave my pen … I wonder if I turned the iron off … I must slow down … I really have to brighten up my act … made a terrible impression last time … damn, forgot the dry-cleaning … I've got to relax … I think I might be getting an ulcer … really should see a doctor … where's all that writing paper … why can't you ever find anything when you need it … I've really got to clean out all these drawers … I'm putting on weight and I don't think I've got enough money to pay the gas bill next week … I've got to relax … ' You just can't turn your mind off. You can't get to sleep. You ignore your diet. Things seem to get worse.

Imagine how calming it would be if you were unaffected by extraneous rubbish and all those unimportant thoughts. Imagine what it would be like if, at will, you could have only one thing on your mind at the one time. Imagine what it would be like to be able to sit down and do just one thing without distraction, without worrying about what you did yesterday or what you have to do tomorrow or what's going on in the next room. Imagine being able to *concentrate*!

Maybe you could even imagine having nothing at all on your mind, on some occasions, for however brief a moment. Wouldn't that be something? Can you just imagine what a calming effect that could have on you?

Centring your mind or attention on just one thing is tantamount to having nothing on your mind at all. You see, it is the very nature of thought to be always on the move. Thought depends on constant movement for its very existence; it is a dynamic process. Thoughts are always coming from one place to go to another; moving from one concept to the next. If, by some means or other, you halt this restless process and the mind is no longer preoccupied with unsolicited thoughts, it soon becomes completely stilled. Only consciousness remains. And when you can achieve an absence of thought, you will begin to know what your mind really is; or more importantly, what your *self* really is.

Contrary to popular opinion, the mind is not the custodian of truth and understanding, it is nothing more than the activity of your consciousness. How many times have you thought your 'mind was playing tricks on you', you were 'fooling yourself', or you'd 'convinced yourself' that something or other was true? If your mind was your real master, and not just an activity of your consciousness, why would you suffer so many ego-related problems? Why would your mind delude you into thinking you were sick when all you really wanted was attention; that you were hungry when in fact you were sad; that you loved when really you lusted; that you disliked wealthy people when in fact you envied them; that you were quite svelte when in fact you were overweight? And if your mind was the supreme authority in your make-up, how could you consciously plan … let alone achieve … a change to your way of thinking (e.g. 'I'm going to force myself to think positively')?

When you control your mind you have the capacity for greatness. When your mind controls you, you are a slave to your ego and your senses. By teaching you how to focus, the Calm Technique will teach you how to quiet your mind and, in doing so, elevate your consciousness.

All this talk of stilling the mind may prompt you to dismiss the Calm Technique as an escapist routine. Nothing could be further from the truth. The meditative process is a discipline which trains you to concentrate your attention and thus improve the efficiency of your thinking. It enhances your understanding and all your intellectual facilities. And, in time, it becomes an extremely reliable way of differentiating between romance and reality.

HAVING ONLY ONE THING ON YOUR MIND

In spite of how easy it may appear to have only one thing on your mind at one time, it is an extraordinarily difficult task. Great athletes can sometimes do it, I'm told. Perhaps great scientists and thinkers can too. But ordinary folk like you and me have to be trained.

If you think I'm exaggerating, try this simple test:

Think of an egg. Just an egg. Nothing more. Not about hens or egg cups or prices. Close your eyes, visualize an egg, and for *two minutes* think only of that egg. With no other thought coming into your mind.

Right, close your eyes.

You thought it was going to be easy, didn't you. You thought of how you had to concentrate. You wondered if you were sitting the right way and whether your two minutes were up. You congratulated yourself on how easy it was. And you probably thought a hundred other thoughts. You see, the human mind finds it almost impossible to concentrate on only one thought for any length of time. Unless it's trained.

Athletes understand this. The heavyweight boxer pounds away at a punching ball for hours on end so that he no longer has to think about punching, so that he will no longer be distracted by the pain and exhaustion. The marathon runner treads the same steps, day in day out, so that she never has to consider the act of running or the pain, but can focus her consciousness on her internal timing clock. You practise the Calm Technique every day of your life so you never have to think about thinking, so you can focus your consciousness on 'being'.

No doubt you've heard of the 'runner's high', where the runner experiences a trance-like state, a great feeling of psychological wellbeing, and moments of deep personal insight. It is the same during the Calm Technique. And other similarities continue: the experienced meditator feels deprived if a day's meditation is missed, just as the runner is frustrated when denied the daily run. Both the meditator and the well-tuned athlete develop an increased capacity to cope with and enjoy life, and by becoming more healthy, eliminate stress from their lives. However, the Calm Technique does it more effectively, and is considerably easier on the feet!

HOW LONG DOES ALL THIS TAKE?

The biggest problem the twentieth century Western student has to overcome is impatience. Western culture and attitudes are geared towards the immediate result, the overnight success. The advertising and magazine mentality of our age, where information is continually telegraphed in short entertaining bursts, and where the spectacular always triumphs over the substantial, has affected our capacity to approach a subject with the depth and determination it often deserves. Our attention spans have been severely reduced. Our ability to persevere with a course of action or thinking, once embarked upon, is similarly affected.

This advertising and magazine mentality has produced a proliferation of self-improvement courses (this one included). Many people have the desire to improve, but lack the willingness to persevere. Consequently they flit from one superficial solution to the next, hoping for an easier way out, a big result for a small involvement, instant success or nirvana. Consequently, many self-improvement devotees tend to fall into extreme categories like the fanatics or the dilettantes.

The Calm Technique does not lend itself to fanaticism; there is insufficient mystery surrounding it. But I fear it could be an ideal playground for the dilettante: it has definite short-term potential where practical results can be realized, and it can also be resurrected with considerable success after long periods of abstinence. But, as the greatest benefits the Calm Technique has to offer are reserved for those who persevere, part-time involvement will only realise a fraction of its true potential. Dedication, perseverance and regular practice will bring profound long-term results which far outweigh any immediate improvements.

The benefits will be obvious from the first time you use the Calm Technique. They may be subtle but, at the very least, they will be relaxing and enjoyable. After a couple of weeks, you'll have a definite feeling of calm and wellbeing, you'll be more at ease with yourself and the world. If you smoke, overeat or drink to excess, you'll probably begin to feel the urge to wean yourself from these bad habits. (**Note:** This is not to suggest that the Calm Technique is a smoking/eating/drinking cure. It can help, but it's not a cure in its own right. Still, as you get more in touch with yourself through the Calm Technique, you'll find it more desirable and much easier to rid yourself of these habits.)

After a few weeks, when the improvements and the benefits aren't as obvious as they were in the first few days, you'll probably start to feel a bit impatient. The standard dilettante approach at this stage is to decide things aren't happening fast enough, and stop or seek yet another 'solution'. But the solution lies in your persistence. There is no meditation or self-improvement technique in existence that will produce dramatic results overnight. The Calm Technique *can* change your life dramatically, but it takes time. As meditation in itself has no goal, it can have no end. At no stage in your life will you ever be able to say, 'I've made it', because the process is ongoing. Like physical exercise, the Calm Technique should be a lifetime commitment.

Before you dismiss all this as too hard, let me give you an assurance. After a month or so of the Calm Technique, you will *want* to make it a lifetime commitment. Every morning and evening for the rest of your life won't seem like a burden, it will seem like a pleasure. You will actually look forward to those rare moments of peace and harmony (relaxation) that modern life seldom offers. And the more you listen to the subtle things your body tells you, the more you will appreciate how important the Calm Technique really is to your life. Ultimately, as the runner becomes addicted to his running, so the meditator becomes addicted to meditation.

How long does it take? A day? A lifetime?

The ideal time to be spent with the Calm Technique each day is fifteen to thirty minutes, morning and evening. Most people seem to spend twenty minutes each time, but you should decide on a time for yourself. After a week, you will know what is the ideal time for you. Then you should standardize. If it's twenty minutes, it should be twenty minutes every time. Because even though the Calm Technique involves no heavy discipline, it *is* a discipline in itself. So regularity, diligence and determination will all bring their own rewards. Please note that the time you spend on the Calm Technique should be governed by how you react to it and what you want to get out of it, and not by what your schedule expects.

To begin with, let's set the standard time for the Calm Technique at twenty minutes. (Later you can vary it a little in either direction to suit the way you feel.) The times of day you should devote to the Calm Technique are once in the morning and once at evening, preferably before meals and as early as your schedule will allow. As the Calm Technique will have you feeling more alert and wide-awake at the end than when you began, it's preferable that your evening meditation takes place a couple of hours before bedtime (although experience will tell whether this is the case with you).

Twenty minutes twice a day will probably seem like quite a chunk out of your day. It is. The compensations are that you will feel much better for having done it in the morning, and you'll sleep better for having done it at night. You'll find that trading half an hour's sleep for half an hour with the Calm Technique is well worth it. Besides, a relaxed person sleeps better and gets by on significantly less sleep than a stressed person.

If the Calm Technique *had* to be performed without fail for twenty minutes twice a day, then it would be a stressbuilder in itself. The ideal is twenty minutes twice a day. But that's all it is, an ideal.

I should emphasize one last time the similarity between the Calm Technique and an exercise programme. You will notice the effect in the first few days. After that, the effects will be gradual and barely discernible, but in the long run, you'll revel in the accumulated benefits of this tuning, training and exercise, and you'll wonder how you ever lived without it.

Even if you have doubts, I sincerely urge you to persist with the Calm Technique for at least two months. After that, you won't need the urging – the benefits will be so obvious to you, you'll never want to stop.

But above all, learn to enjoy and appreciate the time you spend on the Calm Technique for its own sake. Then the long-term benefits to your health and psyche will look after themselves.

The Experience

'Without going out of your door,
you can know all things on earth
Without looking out of your window,
you can know the ways of heaven...
See all without looking.'
George Harrison, 'The Inner Light'

reprinted by kind permission of Northern Songs

WHAT DOES IT FEEL LIKE?

WE'VE LOOKED AT THE PHYSIOLOGICAL
CHANGES that take place during the Calm Technique.
We've looked at the benefits that accumulate through
regular practice. But what is it really like? How does
it feel?

Obviously, different people react in different ways, and for many, the feeling is very difficult to articulate. To ask someone what took place during meditation is the most intimate and personal question a researcher could put forth. Still, in the interests of science, the question has been asked.

There is universal agreement that the most significant feeling is one of great peace and calm. A feeling which, for many, is more peaceful than anything they had ever experienced before. Yet the majority consider that feeling to be strangely familiar, as if they had experienced it before, but couldn't bring it to mind. One man compared it to how he imagined he felt as an infant: loved, safe, no worries, happy, content. Another described it as 'nothingness: empty, floating, detached'. Another as 'radiant'. 'Pure.' 'Not aware that I'm meditating.' 'Sensitive.' 'Aware.' 'Alive.' 'Time stands still.'

There is a place within all of us where, on very rare occasions, we feel completely at peace with existence, completely calm. Let's fantasize for a moment and see if we can recreate just a hint of that feeling. I've listed four scenarios for you to indulge in for your next quiet moment. Select one (or create one of your own), memorize the concept, then close your eyes for a few minutes and try to imagine yourself in that situation.

Do it in some peaceful, dimly lit place.

1) You are an eighteen-month-old infant. You're sitting on your favourite soft blanket in the warm sun. You've found something new to play with and you're totally engrossed in it. So engrossed that you do not bother to look up to see your proud parents standing nearby, beaming. You don't have a worry or a concern in the world; no doubts about the future and no regrets over the past. With you on that blanket is everything you've ever wanted in the world – one scruffy toy.

2) You're a young adult lying on your back in the lush green countryside. Lying beside you is the most important person in your life. You have

nothing to do for the rest of the day. No work to worry about for a couple of weeks. Nothing at all on your mind except how much you are enjoying lying there, without speaking, but sharing the experience. You hear birds some distance away. You stare at the clear blue sky as one lonely cloud slowly passes through the heavens.

3) You have been bushwalking. It has been a very hot day. Ten minutes ago you came upon a beautiful mountain rock pool. The air is cool and moist and refreshing. The water is crystal clear, but very dark. There are cool ferns reflected around its perimeter. The still, clear waters of this pond are mirror-flat except where a gentle waterfall flows, a hundred metres away from you. You are amazed at how calm and still the water is.

4) You are lying on an inflatable mattress on a sheltered South Pacific lagoon. You feel

absolutely safe. There is nothing you have to do. The sun is a trifle too hot, but a gentle breeze keeps you feeling comfortable. There is no possible risk of sunburn. You can hear the water lapping against your inflatable mattress and the shore. Every now and then the shadow of an overhanging coconut tree shelters you from the sun. You are feeling quite drowsy.

Most people find that one of the above fantasies can produce a brief experience of great peace and calm. If you can imagine yourself in one of these situations for however short a time, you will have an inkling of what the Calm Experience feels like (on a superficial level, obviously).

During the Calm Technique, you should feel as peaceful as that. However, at the same time your mind will be fully alert – not thinking, but extremely aware.

In an ideal meditation you would have no recollections and no obvious feelings (either good or bad).

In fact, you would be oblivious to every other thing that's going on in the world, even of the fact that you are only feeling peace and calm at the time. This is not to suggest that you are experiencing 'nothing'. You will be *aware* of everything, just *thinking* about nothing.

However, it will be a long time before your meditation is 'ideal'. As I've said before, the experience is subtle. You will experience moments (sometimes only for a few seconds each time) during the Calm Technique when you are aware of nothing at all, yet you are aware. After it happens you're usually so impressed by your 'achievement' that you begin to congratulate yourself. That congratulatory thought is just another distraction, so you'll have to start over again. But you will appreciate even those brief moments so much that you will continue to be attracted to the Calm Technique. And the more time you dedicate to it, the more those moments of absolute peace and calm will grow. This should not in any way suggest to you that your meditation is limited to the pursuit of these fleeting moments. If you spend twenty minutes on the Calm Technique and only ten seconds result in absolute peace and calm, it does not mean you have wasted nineteen minutes and fifty seconds. The fact that you sit in meditation for twenty minutes (ignoring that wonderful ten seconds) is what produces your sense of calm and strengthens your personality.

The entire twenty minutes should be a time of deep, enjoyable relaxation, a new and completely different experience each time you do it. Expect it to be different. Expect it to be close to perfect sometimes, and almost frustrating at others. Learn to accept it as it comes, be a passive observer. If you try too hard to influence the outcome of your own meditation it becomes counterproductive: you introduce an element of stress into an activity which is meant to be the antithesis of stress.

My explanations of what the Calm Technique 'feels like' must leave something to be desired. It is not an 'experience' as such, it is a state of being. And a state of being cannot be described. You try to describe calm. Or happy. Or love. They are states of being which defy description. You could come up with very creative and poetic sets of words, but the concepts would be meaningless to someone who has never experienced these states.

Perhaps it is more understandable now why 'the best definition of meditation is the act of meditation itself'.

SECTION II

CHAPTER 4

The Technique

'The true lover of knowledge is always striving after being.'
Plato

PREPARATION

NOW WE GET TO THE PART OF THE BOOK where
you actually learn how to use the Calm Technique. From
now on the going gets more practical and much easier to
follow. Nevertheless, I do urge you to ensure you understand each section before going on to the next.

Your first experience of the Calm Technique should
be absolutely right. That doesn't mean you should
approach it with trepidation because there is absolutely
nothing harmful that can happen. The biggest risk is
merely that you have built your expectations (or more

probably, I have built your expectations) too much and you may find it a bit of an anticlimax. So clear your head of all preconceptions and expectations, and expect nothing more than a peaceful, calm, twenty minutes. Expect to feel calm and relaxed when you're finished. Anything else will be a bonus.

I'll say it again. Your first experience should be absolutely right. So any preparation that needs to be done should be done faithfully.

BEFORE YOUR FIRST MEDITATION

1) Avoid alcohol and drugs for at least twenty-four hours before your *first* meditation.
2) Plan it for an occasion when you know you will not be disturbed.
3) Be rested – don't try it after two hours' sleep.
4) Approach it with an open frame of mind.
5) Your expectations should not be too high.
6) You have nothing to fear – you will not lose consciousness or anything sinister like that.

7) No experiments until the text tells you to!

WHERE TO DO IT

As you know, the Calm Technique is a discipline. It is
also habitual. Therefore, it is desirable to practise it
in the same place each time. The same room, the same
corner, the same chair. While this is not essential, you
will find that your special place tends to develop an
aura of great calm for you, and even in moments when
you're not meditating, this place will be a peaceful
retreat for you. (There is nothing magical about this.
You associate a certain place with a feeling of peace
and calm, and you'll feel peace and calm when you're
there. Elementary.) The room should be warm, quiet
and private.

The lights should be low. While it isn't necessary
to have a blacked out room, you'll find that very low
light levels are most helpful in the early stages of
learning the Calm Technique. You'll also find that a
warm-coloured light globe is very relaxing in itself.

If you'd like to try one – especially for your first few meditations – it will help create an atmosphere of calm.

Your chair should be comfortable and reasonably straight backed. As you are not required to adopt any particular physical posture during the Calm Technique, you should seek out a chair that's comfortable. Any kind of chair is suitable, though I prefer the more rigid upright kind, because it prevents drowsiness.

Plant a clock nearby – preferably not a loud-ticking one – where you can refer to it occasionally. To avoid a heart attack, make sure the alarm is turned off. After a couple of times with the Calm Technique, you'll find your body clock has taken over and you'll know exactly when your twenty minutes are up. As long as you don't feel insecure about your own timing ability (in which case you'll be checking with the clock every two minutes), your body will tell you with great accuracy when your time is up.

You could also burn a stick of incense if you wish. It does contribute to the calm atmosphere of your room (and has been known to affect the psycho-neuro centre of the brain).

Finally, take the phone off the hook.

HOW TO PREPARE YOUR ENVIRONMENT

1) Have your own special calm place.
2) Lower the lights; perhaps use a warm coloured globe.
3) Use a straight-backed, comfortable chair.
4) Place a clock nearby if necessary.
5) Use incense if you wish.
6) Take the phone off the hook.

YOUR POSTURE

There is no difficult posture required with the Calm Technique (other than a mental posture, perhaps). As long as your back is reasonably straight and your head up, you'll be fine. Hands and feet can go wherever they feel comfortable.

Make sure you're wearing comfortable clothing. Loose garments, no tight belts, no shoes.

You should be very relaxed before you begin the Calm Technique. If you're suffering nervous feelings, if you're twitchy and fidgety, there are some Calm Exercises (*see pages 124 – 136*) which will relax you. This is very important. *You must begin the Calm Technique in a relaxed frame of mind otherwise you will be overcome with impatience.*

Before you do anything at all, sit for a minute or so until you feel perfectly calm. Your breathing will be slow and regular. You will hear it quite clearly. Forget about everything around you. Forget about the world. Forget about what you have to do in the Calm Technique. Just relax. If you find you have to sit for five minutes before your mind is calm, then do so. It will be worth it.

Initially, you'll practise the Calm Technique with your eyes closed. (In a later version you'll discover an alternative to this. But in most instances, eyes closed.) Your closed eyes should be looking straight ahead, unfocused.

YOUR POSTURE DURING THE CALM TECHNIQUE
1) Back straight, head up.
2) Wear comfortable clothes, no shoes.
3) Be relaxed or do Calm Exercises.
4) Sit for a few moments, breathe regularly.
5) Eyes closed, unfocused, looking straight ahead.

Before we continue with your meditation, there is one note of caution which all meditation teachers give. Meditation should always be approached from a common-sense point of view. If at any stage you 'know' or sense that something is wrong, or something really doesn't feel right, simply stop. Tomorrow things will almost surely be different. This is not to suggest that the Calm Technique is some sort of hallucinogenic or potentially dangerous activity. However, meditation depends upon you feeling 'right', and serves no purpose if it feels 'wrong'. There will be occasions in meditation when you feel fidgety, anxious, scatterbrained, or simply tired. You have these feelings many times a day whether you're meditating or not, so they are completely natural and will occur.

During meditation, trivial annoyances may take on a greater significance than they deserve, simply because they can easily be turned into large and welcome distractions. All teachers recommend that you ignore them.

There is no call for heroics in the Calm Technique. If you're really troubled by something, stop what you're doing and take a break. If you've only just begun the session, try performing the Calm Exercises until you are more relaxed. If, on the other hand, your problem is tiredness, the Calm Exercises should wake you a little. If not, try sleeping. Should you really have something serious on your mind that you find impossible to ignore, don't worry, resume your meditation the following morning or evening. There is no advantage in *forcing* yourself to do anything; that does little more than add to your overall level of anxiety. You should *condition* yourself to have the right frame of mind, to reject distractions, to keep your attention focused on the task. It is this gradual and persistent conditioning (and your willpower) that perfects the Calm Technique. Acts of great intensity and personal sacrifice can be reserved for more deserving occasions like running marathons and saving civilizations.

THE BREATHING MEDITATION

Having read the preparatory chapters, you're no doubt anxious to get the show on the road and try out the Calm Technique. But there is an even simpler meditation than the Calm Technique which is an ideal introduction for you.

It is a simplified, old Zen breathing meditation. In this book its purpose is to provide a comfortable first step into meditation. In practice, this breathing meditation could be an end in itself. You could perform this every day and night for the rest of your life and in the long run it would probably be as beneficial as any other meditation. But it has been simplified and many people find difficulty in sticking with it for any length of time. (Probably because it seems too simple.)

You should begin with this breathing meditation before you start experimenting with the Calm Technique, at least for the first couple of days. Stay with it for as long as you feel comfortable. If you really found it worthwhile, perhaps you should leave well alone and stay with it indefinitely. Whatever you ultimately decide to do, make sure you spend at least a couple of days on this before you move on; contained within the breathing meditation is some of the Calm Technique.

Prepare your environment (*see page 71*) and check your posture (*see page 73*). Now you're ready to begin. The object of the breathing meditation is to be as aware of your breathing as you can. Totally aware. Be aware of nothing else – the fact that you're meditating or whether you're doing it correctly or not – just be aware of your breathing.

Please remember that this is not an exercise in enforced concentration. While you should approach it with determination, you are not meant to force yourself to concentrate. That would not be a relaxing meditation, and you would probably end up feeling more frustrated than when you began.

So, with your eyes closed, mind very still, not thinking about anything at all, slowly begin to bring your mind to rest. Begin to withdraw from and ignore the world about you. Gradually turn your attention inward to your 'self'. Soon you'll hear the sound of your own breathing. Let it become more and more intrusive. Be completely aware of the sound of your breathing. Be aware of the air streaming in through your nostrils, filling your lungs, then being expelled through your lips. Don't try any great feats of lung filling here or you'll hyperventilate. Visualize that stream of cold, fresh air being drawn in through your nostrils. 'See' it being drawn down, deep into your lungs. 'See' that stream of warm air being expelled through your lips. Soon you will be aware only of your breathing. You will *become* your breathing.

When you have reached the stage where breathing is the foremost thought in your mind, forget about it. You will be aware of it, but you should not be thinking about it. Now you begin your breathing meditation.

Count each breath as it leaves your body. Silently count 'one'. When the next breath comes, count 'two'. Then 'three' and 'four'. After 'four' begin at 'one' again and continue this silent count. *Hear* yourself saying each count. Imagine your own counting resounding in your head. (Do this without murmuring a sound, of course.) Count each breath: one, two, three, four, one two … until you become aware only of your counting. Don't think of what you're doing, or the relevance of it, or the meaning of the numbers. It has no meaning, no purpose other than counting four breaths and starting the count all over again.

This continues for fifteen or twenty minutes. Every fibre of your being is involved in this one thing, and you are doing it completely.

It may become obvious to you that the content of this meditation – the meaning of the numbers and the counting – is, in itself, quite meaningless. But the fact that you are doing only one thing at the one time is the point of the exercise. The counting is nothing more than a technique for centring your attention. (In Zen training, the count is to ten. It's more difficult, but you can do it that way if you feel up to it.) You may become aware of the fact that your breathing has slowed to less than you would have previously considered normal. This is probably true, but should be dismissed as irrelevant and nothing but a distraction. You may become aware of the fact that you can't remember ever having felt so relaxed and peaceful. This, too, is irrelevant and has nothing to do with your meditation. You may also think that you're doing very well at your breathing meditation – this thought means you are not doing it as well as is possible.

It won't be long before your mind starts to wander and you'll begin thinking of various things. A long while before you notice it, you will have forgotten your counting and will be thinking of something entirely different. When you become aware of this happening, calmly redirect your thinking to your counting. This is not meant to be a contemplation of counting. Don't treat it too seriously; the wandering mind is part of meditation. Just be aware of the fact that you have strayed from your course, and calmly lead yourself back on to the true path – your counting.

Remember, don't force yourself to concentrate. You should approach the breathing meditation in the most relaxed way possible. If you're faced with the choice of being relaxed with distracting thoughts, or anxious through forcing yourself to concentrate, choose the relaxation path. Sooner or later you will be able to direct your awareness back to your counting *with a minimum of fuss*. If you manage to count only four breaths before your mind wanders, it is all right.

Next time it might be four sets of four. But don't get competitive with yourself; the goal is to be counting, not to be able to count to four 'x' times.

Soon you will find (and if you are meditating well, you will be unaware of this fact) that thoughts are no longer distracting you; that your counting is everything and is dominating your consciousness. You will soon become, as they say, 'one with your counting'. When this happens, you will have a clarity of understanding that the wandering mind is incapable of experiencing.

At the end of this meditation, sit quietly for a minute or two until you readjust. Reflect on the past twenty minutes, on what you felt, on how you feel at the moment. You should have experienced a few moments of absolute calm. You should feel completely relaxed. You will also be aware of just how difficult it is to do only one thing at a time. You may be tempted to think you're not very good at this meditation business. However, distraction is very much a part of meditation. Everyone gets distracted. But if you spent the entire twenty minutes being distracted, it probably means that you weren't properly prepared. You have to develop a relaxed frame of mind before you begin, your meditation builds on that. If at any time you feel your meditation has been unsuccessful, it doesn't matter. Each meditation is unique; some live up to your expectation of good, some do not. The fact that you meditated at all makes it 'good'.

THE BREATHING MEDITATION

1) Prepare your environment. Check posture.
2) Close eyes, relax.
3) Focus on your breath entering and leaving your body.
4) Count breaths one to four, repeat.
5) Don't fight a wandering mind, but calmly direct it back to the task.
6) Sit for a minute afterwards.

You can repeat the Breathing Meditation every morning and evening for at least a few days. Ideally, it should be for a month or so, unless you're impatient to get on with the Calm Technique. But bear in mind, if you decide you feel comfortable with this breathing meditation, stay with it. Any meditation done consistently will work.

THE TECHNIQUE

The Calm Technique, like the Breathing Meditation, is a 'structured' meditation. This means there is a set procedure for you to follow, and it requires a moderate amount of determination and discipline to be successful. For many, the mere mention of the word 'discipline' brings with it visions of deprivation, hard work and sacrifice. It should be stressed that this is not the case with the Calm Technique. We have already learned that in this type of meditation you avoid concentration and extreme effort, because no amount of human determination by itself can produce such a natural and peaceful state as the Calm State.

You may have heard of some meditation techniques which require 'no discipline at all'. These techniques should be afforded the same seriousness that you would give to a smoking cure which required no willpower, a fitness programme that involved no exercise, a money-making scheme that involved no risk or effort. If there were such magic programmes, then *everybody* would be healthy, rich, nonsmokers. Let me assure you that every successful form of meditation requires determination, application and a degree of discipline. The Calm Technique is no exception.

The only discipline required for the Calm Technique is that you practise it regularly and that you *work at* having only one thing on your mind at the one time. At no stage do you have to *force* yourself to concentrate or to think a certain way.

As a structured meditation, the Calm Technique requires you to follow a specified path of action (mental activity). Later, we will learn of modifications to this technique, but initially, there is an established route for you to follow. It is similar to one of the most well-known and popular routes in the world today: the mantra meditation.

THE HISTORY OF THE MANTRA

If we were to review meditation by technique alone, the Calm Technique would appear to have much in common with a type of meditation that Indian Yogis have been using for over three thousand years (as taught by Shri Shankaracharya). The methods and attitudes it was based on probably evolved even earlier. This same method was used in ancient Judaic meditation, as well as some of the early Christian ones.

The core of this method was a single word or phrase, which in the Indian tradition was called the mantra. It was intuitively conceived by a teacher or guru and passed on to a student or disciple who used it exclusively as the major part of his or her meditation. Although it was permissible for this mantra to be *any* sound or phrase, it was often a Sanskrit* word or words from the Vedic hymns which form the basis of Hindu scripture.

The mantra was usually a single word or expression, or a complete prayer which was considered to be of great spiritual significance.

That is the classic application of the mantra. The mantra *type* of meditation (also known as 'Japa' or 'Japam') has been in constant use throughout the centuries by communities and sects who knew nothing of Sanskrit. Even though some non-Indian countries, such as China and Japan, often used Sanskrit mantras, most chose their mantras from their own languages, a practice that is still followed today.

For a Hindu, a Sanskrit mantra may be important. For a Westerner, where the opportunity of receiving the perfect Sanskrit word or phrase is a rather remote

*Sanskrit is a sacred language that was used in north-west India about 1500 BC.

possibility, it has negligible importance. Where there is no cultural affinity with a language, however 'sacred' it may be, no great benefit to be derived from using it.

Ancient tradition also dictated that a mantra should be passed from teacher to student. Some sects today place quite a lot of emphasis on 'personal' mantras. Such a mantra is claimed to have been specially divined for an individual, often for a fee. Even though the results are successful, there is a fair amount of mystical show business and commercialism involved in the process. I very much doubt whether any Western teacher of a few years' experience can pluck a Sanskrit word out of either thin air or the Vedas to give you a mantra with more cosmic properties than one you would have chosen from your own humble English dictionary.

I remember once, as a child, being invited to a Catholic chapel for evening prayer. There were about 200 young men and boys in there reciting 'the Rosary', which incidentally, takes about twenty minutes, the same as the Calm Technique. I consider this my first practical demonstration of meditation, where the constant repetition of some wellworn phrases (mantra) managed to banish everything from the mind and elevate the consciousness in a way that I now associate with the experience of the Calm Technique. While it would never be described as such in theological circles, the Rosary functions as a type of mantra.

Some of the more well-known mantras you may have heard of are 'Om' (or 'Aum' as it's often spelt), 'Hare Krishna', 'Lord Jesus Christ, son of God, have mercy upon me a sinner' (the mantra of early Christian monks), 'Kyrie Eleison' (Latin), 'Allah al akbar' (Arabic). There are millions of them being used very effectively every day.

The mantra type of meditation is widely used today. It is recognized in all schools as being one of the more effective methods available, and has certainly been the one which has enjoyed the most success in the Western world.

CALM EXPRESSIONS

Some medical experiments have shown that the physiological responses of subjects who had used the 'spiritually superior' type of mantras were just as pronounced when the subjects meditated with nonsensical words provided at random by scientists controlling the experiments. Of course this is no measure of the spiritual qualities of those mantras, nor is it for us to question the spiritual worth of disciplines which have evolved over thousands of years. However, as the Calm Technique is concerned mainly with the temporal (physical, mental and emotional) aspects, the origins of the mantra are less important. As far as the Calm Technique is concerned, the meaning of the mantra has about as much inherent significance to the meditator as the colour of the barbell does to the weightlifter.

Nevertheless, should you feel compelled to follow tradition, buy a copy of the *Bhagavad-gita* next time you pass a Hare Krishna. It has pages of Sanskrit words you could choose from.

The Calm Technique aims to provide a practical method of relaxation and meditation that will benefit the Western reader. It employs a non-mystical device, similar to the mantra, called a Calm Expression. In application, the literal content of the Calm Expression is just as meaningful, or just as meaningless, as counting one, two, three, four, one, two, etc., as we do in the Breathing Meditation. The repetitive use of the word, or phrase, is all that's important; the meaning is irrelevant.

What is important about *your* Calm Expression is that you select a word or phrase and persist with it. After you have adopted one – regardless of its origin – there is no reason whatsoever for changing it. You should, unless you have good reason not to, stay with it forever. Furthermore, the word or phrase should remain personal and internal when you begin using it. It should be something between you and the inner recesses of your mind, and therefore, not something to be discussed.

You will find that in time, your Calm Expression will take on a meaning (only to you) far in excess of its literal interpretation. The time will come when even its fleeting occurrence in your mind will be sufficient to trigger a subconscious reaction that will relax you, that will make you feel more calm, that will remind you of how calm it is possible to be when meditating. And when you have used a Calm Expression for some time, it will take on calming properties that you would never have thought possible from a single word; it will be your personal refuge from stress and anxiety that you can have with you all day.

Now it is time for you to select your Calm Expression.
If you belong to some particular faith or religion, you may choose a word or a simple phrase which relates to your beliefs. In most cases, I would suggest using a word which lacks meaning, or one which has a simple comforting meaning. You can use any word or sound in

existence as long as you feel comfortable with it. You needn't be concerned with what others will think of it, because you need never discuss your choice with another human being. If you have concerns about making the wrong choice, I suggest you use the word 'calm-ing'. Even if you ignore the meaning (which you will), it has a beautiful calming sound and effect. Please bear in mind though, that the meaning of the word is not important. All that's important is that you adopt a Calm Expression and stay with it.

Have you chosen one? If you haven't, use 'calm-ing'. Now you're ready to apply it.

THE CALM CENTRE

There is a place within all of us which we recognize as the very core of our being. To most modern thinkers, this would probably be the brain. To the ancient Egyptians (and later the Greeks and Romans), it was the heart or the liver. In other parts of the world it has variously been described as being located at the base of the spine, the pit of the belly, the pituitary gland (in nineteenth-century England) and the hypothalamus (to Indians, the Ajna Chakra). It is this latter area which concerns us.

The hypothalamus (*see figure 1*) is an extraordinary part of the brain. In some Eastern sects, it is considered to be the seat of the soul. It sits directly behind where many ancient orders claim the 'Third Eye' is located. (The Third Eye is an 'eye' which metaphorically opens during certain kinds of meditation when the real eyes are closed.) Those who consider the soul to be located at the hypothalamus visualize it as a point of light in the middle of the forehead. (Place a finger at the very top of your nose at your forehead between your eyes. Your hypothalamus is about 7– 9 cm back from that point.)

The hypothalamus also has great significance in modern studies of stress. It is the hypothalamus which spontaneously releases corticotrophin-releasing hormone (CRH) into your pituitary gland when you are confronted by threat or excitement, which in turn releases hormones into the bloodstream. This sets your adrenal glands pumping, which speeds up your pulse and breathing rate. It also suspends your metabolism and generally prepares you for that 'fight or flight' syndrome we considered earlier. So the hypothalamus is central to your rising blood pressure and stress levels.

However, while the hypothalamus may be responsible for the creation of your stress symptoms, it is also the centre which *reverses* the procedure. Not only does it activate physiological responses, it also inhibits them. It is the hypothalamus that decreases the heart rate, lowers the blood pressure, controls body temperature, and monitors metabolism. It is the hypothalamus that maintains your state of alertness or wakefulness, and controls the psychosomatic influences on your health. It is the hypothalamus that controls all of the physiological functions which decide whether you are troubled or at peace. In conjunction with the cerebrum and limbic system, it controls the emotions, perceptions and a whole host of other mental functions. In short, the hypothalamus is the junction and most important link between the mind and the body; it is the very centre of your consciousness! It should not be too great a conceptual leap for you to accept the hypothalamus as your Calm Centre. Not only does it control and activate all the mechanisms which produce the Calm State; not only is it the junction of all your emotions, thoughts and decisions; it is also the one place where you can experience true calm and peace. While the existence of such a place is obviously beyond conventional sensory perception, most of us recognize that there is a natural refuge and haven within each and every one of us which cannot be explained in scientific or psychophysical terms. This is your Calm Centre.

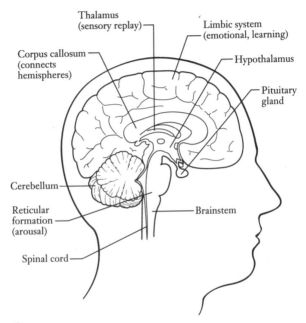

Thalamus
(sensory replay)

Limbic system
(emotional, learning)

Corpus callosum
(connects
hemispheres)

Hypothalamus

Pituitary
gland

Cerebellum

Reticular
formation
(arousal)

Brainstem

Spinal cord

figure 1

LOCATION OF THE HYPOTHALAMUS

Your Calm Centre is uncomplicated. It doesn't know anxiety, fear, frustration, suspicion, doubt, envy. It is at peace with the world, with existence. It is beyond your everyday emotions, thought processes and mental functions. This is the centre that you come in touch with during the Calm Technique; this is where your Calm Expression emanates from.

I must stress that accurate pinpointing of your Calm Centre is unnecessary. What is important is that your Calm Expression emerges from deep within your consciousness, from a place which is *beyond* thought. Then, instead of trying to blank out your undisciplined thoughts through sublimation, you can ignore them and focus your awareness on your Calm Expression. Before you know it, your distractions will be forgotten, your mind will be filled with your Calm Expression and you will be meditating.

Think of your mind as a noisy room full of shouting people. Among all that cacophony is a voice (your Calm Expression) that you recognize. Even though that one voice may be no louder than any other in the room, it can begin to stand out clearly against all others simply because you are interested in that one voice, and because you choose to listen to only one voice.

Think how easily one word can leap out and rivet your attention as you flick through the pages of a book. If you had really concentrated on every word on the page and tried to find it in that moment, you almost certainly wouldn't have seen it. Yet a non-concentrated glance at the pages as you flick through makes it stand out every time.

The Calm Expression which emanates from your Calm Centre behaves similarly. If it appears of its own accord in its own good time, it will dominate your attention much more successfully than if you force yourself to think about it. It will *charm* you into the Calm State, rather than force you into it. By not concentrating, you make it stand out all the more. Although a straightforward disciplined concentration will work, it is much more difficult to perform than the relaxed, passive, non-concentration approach.

If you can generally imagine where your Calm Centre is located, you'll know where your Calm Expression should originate. It will originate of its own accord. It requires no effort on your part at all except being aware of its origins and adopting a completely passive state of mind. The Calm Technique continues from there. Once you have begun, it does require some effort to prevent your attention from straying, however.

If you find all that discussion of the Calm Centre confusing, don't be distressed. It is merely a way of enhancing the *beginning* of your meditation; it is not an integral part of the Calm Technique itself. The Calm Technique is inherently simple, all you have to do is one thing, and do it totally. This will centre your attention and elevate your consciousness. This is the Calm Technique.

USING THE CALM TECHNIQUE

The Calm Technique is nothing more than a constant repetition of the word you have adopted as your Calm Expression. You might think that the repetition of a single word for twenty minutes or more sounds frightfully boring. However, remember that you will not be *thinking* about it, even though you will be *conscious* of it. After a short while, you will cease to take any notice of the word at all, except that you are saying it in your mind.

We're now ready to put into practice all we've learned. Go through the preparatory steps again.

THE ENVIRONMENT

1) Have your own special Calm place.
2) Lower the lights; perhaps use a warm coloured globe.
3) Use a straight-backed, comfortable chair.
4) Place a clock nearby if necessary.
5) Use incense if you wish.
6) Take the phone off the hook.

THE POSTURE

1) Back straight, head up.
2) Wear comfortable clothes, no shoes.
3) Be relaxed or do Calm Exercises.
4) Sit for a few moments, breathe regularly.
5) Eyes closed, unfocused, looking straight ahead.

(We will assume that your Calm Expression is 'calming'. If it is something different, substitute that word or phrase instead of 'calm-ing'.)

When you are perfectly relaxed and not thinking of anything in particular, begin to listen to the sound of your own breathing. Hear that stream of cool air as it is drawn in through your nostrils, deep down into your lungs. Hear it as your body expels its warm breath. Be conscious only of your breathing. Hear only the sound of air passing in through your nostrils, entering your body, being breathed out. With each breath you take, you will become more relaxed. The sound of your own breath will be the most relaxing sound you have ever heard. Don't be alarmed if your breathing sounds slower than you think is normal; that is the process of meditation. Think only of your breathing, of air coming in through your nostrils, deep into your lungs, out through your mouth. Try not to think of what meditation is meant to feel like (you can think about that when you've finished), think only of your breathing. Your breath will be all you hear, all you are conscious of.

Around this time, you will begin to 'hear' your Calm Expression. You should 'hear' it in your own (unspoken) voice, sounding like it's coming from your Calm Centre, deep within your mind. Let it rise to your mind's surface, clearing away other thoughts as it does. Don't try to force other thoughts away by concentration – let your Calm Expression sweep them away – let it dominate your entire consciousness *from within*. There is no time frame on when your Calm Expression should appear. It will almost certainly happen of its own accord (particularly as you grow more familiar with it) after a minute or two, when you are completely relaxed. As well, you will *sense* the right kind of rhythm for the repetition of your Calm Expression. Rhythm is also something that happens of its own accord; it is perfectly all right as long as you don't wonder whether it's right or wrong.

Without uttering a sound, just keep 'hearing' that word over and over again in your mind, until you are aware of nothing else. Until your entire consciousness is filled with your Calm Expression. Don't try to visualize it as a written word, don't try to think about the meaning of the word, and don't try to attribute any special meanings to it. It is, as we've already said, a meaningless device (which will take on a special importance as you make it yours) to direct your consciousness, to discipline your mind. Just go with the flow of your consciousness, be completely passive to what is happening and be totally absorbed by the calming repetition of this word or phrase.

All this talk of 'hearing' a sometimes meaningless word or phrase coming from the inner recesses of your mind shouldn't be intimidating. You are not playing tricks on your mind or sublimating your awareness. Nor are you seeking 'nothingness' or a blank mind (although occasionally you will experience this pleasant phenomenon). What you are seeking to achieve is an absence of random and unnecessary thought by centring your attention on only one thing at one time. When it is focused, you will be calm. When your attention is all over the place, flitting from one thought to the next, concentrating on two things at once, being distracted by every trivial thing that comes along, it functions at a very reduced level.

There are no prizes for cleverness or originality in the Calm Technique. The only prize comes with being able to *charm* your consciousness into being totally involved with your Calm Expression. Please remember this is not an exercise in self-discipline. You don't have to force yourself to concentrate, nor do you have to go to great lengths to 'hear' this meaningless phrase. Be passive. Go with the flow. If your mind begins to wander, calmly redirect it to its task. When distractions come, ignore them and go back to 'hearing' your Calm Expression.

Were you to speak your Calm Expression out loud, you would 'hear' it quite easily. This could make focusing on it a much simpler task because you would note the distractions more clearly when your voice stopped. If you believe you can chant away by yourself every day and evening without having everyone think you're some sort of crank, go right ahead. You'll find it makes the Calm Technique even easier. Nevertheless, you'll almost certainly find that you'll co-exist better with neighbours and the rest of the household if you perform the Calm Technique silently. You decide.

By applying all your consciousness to this one task – the repetition of your Calm Expression – you will soon be lulled into a wonderfully relaxed but surprisingly aware state. If you could maintain your Calm Expression at the forefront of your attention, you would be in a blissful state in no time. But you will be distracted by uninvited thoughts and concepts. Your mind will wander. This is completely natural and expected. When it happens, bring your attention back to your Calm Expression and let that one word soothe all your distractions and anxieties. Let it take you to that place within yourself where there is absolute peace. Let it make you more calm and serene every time you 'hear' it.

You will probably begin to wonder if you're doing everything right. If you forget about wondering and concentrate only on your Calm Expression, you will be doing everything right. Then you will probably begin to wonder if you're experiencing what you're supposed to experience. Or you may even begin to think that meditation is not going to work for you, that you're a 'bad subject'. Once again, if you simply stop wondering and concentrate only on the task at hand, you will be experiencing what you're supposed to, and will be meditating correctly. If you become aware that your attention has wandered, redirect it to your Calm Expression. 'Hear' it being repeated quietly in your mind. Each time you hear it, you will experience an even greater feeling of peace. Of calm. If you begin to think there must be more to meditation than this, return to your meditation. The fact that you're thinking of something other than your Calm Expression means you still have a way to go with your meditation.

By this stage of the Calm Technique, you will be aware of a deep sense of calm and peace. When you've *finished* meditating, you can look back on this feeling. It will not have been something that takes your breath away, more something that felt so totally natural. Many people describe this as one of the first really natural experiences of their adult life.

You may think you should be experiencing something more. But the fact that you're thinking other things at all (during the Calm Technique) is influencing both the experience and the effectiveness of your meditation. Your attention is meant to be centred on your Calm Expression, not what you're feeling. You're meant to be doing just one thing, and doing it totally;

not thinking about what you're doing or how you're progressing. That one thing is 'hearing' your Calm Expression emanating from the Calm Centre within your consciousness. Its constant repetition gradually clears the mind of all thoughts and distractions until finally there comes a moment when your mind is still. (Of course, if at that stage you think, 'Hey, I've done it,' you're back to square one.) When your attention is fully occupied with your Calm Expression, all compulsive, random thinking is overcome and a great sense of calm will arise. This will be your first awareness of true inner peace and contentment.

If you have been able to restrict your thoughts to your Calm Expression, you will be amazed at how quickly twenty minutes can pass. Then, at the end of this period, slowly bring your attention back to the everyday.

Sit a while. Think over how you feel, how you felt. If nothing else, you will be aware of a deep sense of calm and peace. For however brief a moment during the Calm Technique, you would have tasted real peace. Even when those moments of peace are just fleeting glimpses of a higher form of consciousness, they are moments that can have the most extraordinary calming influence over your whole day. And in time, over your whole life.

If at any stage you find it absolutely impossible to keep your Calm Expression in mind, don't let it bother you. Most people will only succeed for a few seconds in the early stages. Just listen to your breathing and enjoy the peace of doing absolutely nothing for a while until you can resume 'hearing' your Calm Expression. This is still meditation. On the other hand, if you find yourself deeply troubled about something, perhaps work pressures or family problems, postpone your meditation until you have a more ordered frame of mind. Then do the Calm Exercises before you begin.

As you can see, the Calm Technique is incredibly simple to perform. The paradox is that its simplicity is also its difficulty. Ironically, the principal problem you will experience is just accepting how very simple it really is. The human mind thrives on distraction and drama, it convinces you that there is no such thing as a 'simple' experience. It urges you to believe that you must make a greater intellectual contribution than you do. How can you experience a higher form of consciousness by employing less of your intellect? How can you improve your capacity for thinking by employing no thoughts? Only experience in the Calm Technique will fully answer these questions for you. Until you can recognize and accept this experience in its own right, you need only understand that your intellect and ego are self-supporting parts of the same. The combined might of these two elements makes it very difficult for you to appreciate any higher consciousness, especially a higher consciousness that can only be attained by transcending their influence altogether. Yet, when you are no longer distracted by the prattle of uninvited thoughts, when you can transcend your own ego and intellect, you will know otherwise.

THE CALM TECHNIQUE

1) Create the right environment.
2) Adopt the correct posture.
3) Listen to your breathing. Let it relax you with each breath.
4) 'Hear' your Calm Expression emanate from your Calm Centre. 'Hear' it repetitively in your mind.
5) When thoughts distract, gently turn the attention back to your Calm Expression.
6) Don't worry about whether you're doing it right.
7) Sit in contemplation for a few moments when you're finished.

Let me assure you one more time of the simplicity of the Calm Technique. Approach it with an open mind and it will have a positive influence in your life. Dismiss your preconceptions and, within a few weeks, your own experience will tell you that it has been worth the effort.

THE OBSTACLES

Because the Calm Technique is such an uncomplicated,
easy-to-understand exercise, the major problem most
people experience is believing it could possibly be so
simple. It can. In fact, once you can accept its ease and
simplicity, there should be only two other obstacles
you will have to contend with: unwanted thoughts
and impatience.

UNWANTED THOUGHTS

In the West, where meditation is generally associated
with religious thinking and prayer, a vivid imagination
and lively thought processes are highly prized. In the
East, and in schools where meditation is used to enrich
everyday life, the thinking process is viewed with much
less reverence. Thoughts are often considered to be
mere distractions and a hindrance to effective meditation. With the Calm Technique, for example, the prize
is the *absence* of uninvited thoughts, imagination and

sensory perceptions. And it is towards this end that the Calm Technique is devoted. It is not the Calm Expression, or the posture, or the frame of mind which produces this wonderful calming influence and expansion of awareness, it is the absence of unrelated thought brought about by centring the attention.

But is that not an escapist ideal? Aren't we over-looking the majesty of the mind? Is not the mind really the person?

Most of us tend to think of ourselves as the product of our minds and our mental attitudes. Yet it is these very mental attitudes which limit our development as human beings. How often have you wished you could think another way, that you could have stronger willpower, that you could convince yourself there was no reason to feel anxious when there was no reason to feel anxious?

You've heard it said many times that all of us only use a tiny part of our mind/brain (meaning consciousness), and that if we could ever realize its full potential, great things could be achieved. The purpose of the Calm Technique is to expand your awareness way beyond the boundaries of your conventional way of thinking and imagination. But first you have to learn to control your thought processes, to train your mind. To elevate your consciousness. You are probably well aware that there are areas of your consciousness which do not function in the usual 'verbal' or 'visual' way. Words such as 'intuition' spring to mind, where you 'sense' something that is beyond the scope of your normal sensory organs. Or 'inspiration', where no matter how hard you try, you cannot satisfactorily verbalize or visualize this experience.

So, during the Calm Technique, the normal workings of your mind continue, but they do not dominate your consciousness. They cease to be the totality of your awareness. During such an activity not only do you enjoy the Calm State, but you have access to regions of your consciousness which you may never have known existed. The Calm Technique will eventually lead you past the boundaries of conventional thinking and imagination, where you will discover a whole new world of peace, creativity, insight and wisdom.

Nevertheless, you will be distracted along the way. You will encounter more uninvited (and probably irrelevant) thoughts than you would think possible. You will also be discomforted by every little itch, twitch and urge under the sun. You will hear things, smell things and feel things that you would normally never notice. These are the distractions of the Calm Technique. They are completely natural and happen to everyone. They exist because the mind does not want to be quietened. It enjoys being master, and will use every possible diversion to retain its superiority and to distract you from your task. The mind does not take kindly to this Calm Technique stuff. But your response to this should be simply to acknowledge that this condition is entirely normal and predictable. Just be passively aware of these thoughts and itches as they come and go, and let them exist quietly in some little corner of your brain. Don't entertain them. Don't be seduced by them. Ignore them. And if they do make their presence felt, calmly turn your attention back to your Calm Expression. Let it dominate all distractions that come your way.

There may be times when your thoughts will be more serious. Perhaps you have work or home problems, financial worries, a speech to deliver in an hour, a wedding. On occasions like this it's probably better for you to give in. If you are really anxious and concerned, your mind will continually turn to your problem rather than the Calm Expression. Although the Calm Technique will eventually be an effective and calming relief from such tensions, in the early stages your resolve will probably not overcome the distraction. Better to postpone your meditation till evening or the following morning.

On occasions when you are greatly distracted by physical discomfort such as an itch or cramp or pins-and-needles, I believe it's usually better to give in, have your scratch, and get on with the job. It is possible to continue until the discomfort passes, but great sacrifices aren't required for the Calm Technique.

Always bear in mind *the object is to teach yourself how to centre your attention, not to force yourself to*. The most effective results are gained when you can guide your wandering mind away from distraction by applying your Calm Expression, not by sublimating your thoughts.

IMPATIENCE

One of the most damaging characteristics of stress is impatience. The condition many people set out to overcome through the Calm Technique can often be the very source of their failure.

Recognize that stress produces a number of nervous conditions such as the apparent inability to cope, lack of concentration, listlessness, fatigue or hyperactivity, irritability and impatience. Like stress itself, these conditions cannot be willed away, or even concealed for any length of time; they are most persistent when they are least needed. As a relaxed, peaceful and non-urgent activity, the Calm Technique is a natural target for impatience. If you are severely stress-affected, impatience will probably be present in your early meditations. In the first week or so, before your stress levels have reduced significantly, you may find impatience getting the better of you. You will complain that things aren't happening fast enough. You will search for short cuts. You may even seek out other means of achieving your ends. But you will be succumbing to one of the maladies you had hoped the Calm Technique would cure.

The truth is that the Calm Technique will triumph over impatience. The issue is how long it will take. It varies, obviously; but the longer you are with the Calm Technique, the less you will be affected by stress symptoms. For some, the improvement is both immediate and very noticeable. For others, it is more progressive and requires much more perseverance, particularly in the early stages. What is important is that you recognize stress exists, accept that it can be eliminated, and be constantly on guard against its negative effects. As time passes, so does impatience.

CHAPTER 6

The Calm Exercises

'Life is so short, the craft so long to learn.'
Hippocrates

THERE WILL BE TIMES when it is almost impossible to sit down and relax in preparation for the Calm Technique. These are the instances when the mind and/or emotions are working overtime on some issue or another. Whether it's a time of great stress and anxiety, or a time of great excitement, or even a simple business problem that requires an immediate answer, you'll find it extremely difficult to attend to the Calm Technique with the attention it deserves. On occasions like this, you should perform the Calm Exercises before you begin. You may find that they never become necessary. However, they should still be learned and considered as an effective and enjoyable introduction to a Calm Technique session. Whether you have need for them or not, you will find the Calm Exercises to be a relaxing interlude in their own right.

The Calm Exercises which follow are derived from Tai Chi. You will almost certainly have seen exhibitions of this graceful, balletic and very relaxing exercise. Although it is well promoted as a *physical* exercise, Tai Chi is an excellent way of meditation. The complex moves demand total attention, and this, as you know, contains the makings of meditation.

The Calm Exercises are not exercises in the traditional callisthenic mould. They are not designed to quicken your heartbeat, trim your waistline or build your stamina. The Calm Exercises have but one purpose: to relax you physically and mentally, so you can effectively use the Calm Technique.

They are incredibly simple to use. In fact, the only thing about the Calm Exercises that you could possibly find difficult is curbing your impatience. They must be done extremely slowly. Unlike any physical exercise you have ever participated in before, Calm Exercises gain in effectiveness the slower they can be performed.

Each exercise is accompanied by a slow breath in, followed by a slow breath out. Each movement relates to either the inhalation or the exhalation of the breath. The slowness of the movement is governed by the slowness of your breathing. The object is to slow your movements and your breathing as much as you comfortably can *without strain*.

As these Calm Exercises depend upon good, natural breathing, it is best to do them near an open window, in the garden or on the balcony. (Don't worry about being noticed; these are very subtle exercises.) They should take five to fifteen minutes to complete.

However, before you begin the Calm Exercises, there are three things you should attend to: your countenance, your stance and your breathing.

TO RELAX YOUR COUNTENANCE

1) Lightly push your tongue against the roof of your mouth just behind your front teeth (this relaxes and unclamps your jaw).

2) Lift your eyebrows very slightly as if you're wide awake (this is to relax the muscles in your eyes and forehead).

3) Have a hint of a smile on your face (this relaxes all the facial muscles).

In Tai Chi and many of the Asian martial arts, your basic stance is one which 'glues' you firmly to the floor so you cannot be thrown off balance. The same stance applies to the Calm Exercises.

TO RELAX YOUR STANCE

1) *Both feet should point straight ahead, a comfortable shoulder-width distance apart.*

2) *All joints should be 'unlocked': knees bent ever so slightly, a slight kink in your elbows, arms not quite touching your body (a little space under your armpits), fingers separated and hands hanging loosely (they'll feel limp and heavy), neck relaxed, head up and looking straight ahead,* back straight.

3) *Slowly concentrate all your weight down through your feet into the floor. Feel your feet becoming heavier and heavier. Feel your weight sinking through your feet, down into the floor.*

Breathing is one of the most important elements of the Calm Technique and the Calm Exercises. Your breath should be as even as possible. Draw in and breathe out in one flowing stream (in other words, don't hold on to your breath before exhaling).

BREATHING

1) *Place your fingers gently on your stomach about four centimetres below your navel.*

2) *Inhale deeply through your nose, slowly and evenly until you can feel your abdomen swell under your fingers (the Chinese call this your* tan tien*). Don't strain. Don't allow your chest to rise. You want a natural, effortless flow of breath into your* tan tien.

3) *Exhale slowly and evenly until you feel your abdomen fall.*

4) *Repeat the slow inhalation, followed by the slow exhalation, with no pauses between.*

5) *Breathe in and out, in and out, five times.*

CALM EXERCISE ONE

This is extremely simple. It is intended as a warm-up exercise for Calm Exercises Two, Three and Four, and as such does not require slow movements. It relaxes the entire top half of your body, and with slight modification, the lower half as well.

1) *Countenance and stance as specified.*
2) *Let your arms hang loose until they feel heavy and relaxed.*
3) *Keeping feet, legs and waist very steady, swing the top half of your body to the left so your shoulders and head are also facing the left. Your arms will wrap loosely around your body as you do so. Then repeat the action to the right. Develop this swinging motion one way, then the other. Your arms will follow the upper part of your body as you pivot from the waist; they will wrap around one way, then swing back the other – always swinging loosely, fingers relaxed.*

4) *Swing one way, then the next, until the weight of your arms is sufficient to turn your body.*

5) Optional: *As one arm passes in front of (the other will be behind) your body, you can bend your knees a few centimetres to create a pumping action as well as a swinging motion. This improves circulation to the lower part of your body.*

6) *Continue for two minutes.*

7) *Gradually slow down the movement until your arms hang loosely by your side again.*

8) *Relax.*

CALM EXERCISE TWO

This is a very simple exercise which should be performed *as slowly as you possibly can.*

1) *Countenance and stance as specified, arms hanging loosely by your side.*
2) *Looking straight ahead, breathe in.*
3) *Slowly turn your head to look back over your left shoulder as you breathe out.*
4) *Breathe in as you bring your head back slowly to face the front.*
5) *Slowly turn your head to look back over your right shoulder as you breathe out.*
6) *Repeat about three times to either side.*

   Now for the second part:
1) *Looking straight ahead, breathe in.*
2) *Exhale as your chin is lowered slowly on to the chest.*
3) *Breathe in as your head comes up straight.*

4) *Exhale as your head is lowered slowly back (so you are looking towards the ceiling).*

5) *Repeat three times forwards and backwards.*

And the third:

1) *Looking straight ahead, breathe in.*

2) *Exhale as you slowly incline your head to the left (facing forwards).*

3) *Breathe in as you bring your head back to the upright position.*

4) *Exhale as you slowly incline your head to the right (still facing forwards).*

5) *Repeat about three times to either side.*

6) *Relax.*

CALM EXERCISE THREE

This is a simple exercise where the arms describe a large circular movement as you rise up on your toes. You breathe in as your arms and your lungs are at their widest. There is nothing tricky about this exercise; if you move your arms in a large circle, your breathing will coordinate naturally. It should be performed *as slowly as you possibly can*.

1) *Countenance and stance as specified.*
2) *Bend knees slightly until almost bow-legged. Elbows bent, wrists crossed about navel level, palms facing upwards* (see figure 2).
3) *As arms move upwards in wide, circular motion, breathe in, straighten legs and rise on to toes as arms reach the highest part of their arc* (see figure 3).
4) *Continue the circular movement as you exhale and let knees bend again* (back to figure 2).
5) *Repeat this movement five times.*

6) *Reverse the whole procedure for another five times.*
7) *Relax.*

figures 2 and 3
CALM EXERCISE 3

CALM EXERCISE FOUR

This exercise is slightly more complex, but the most graceful and relaxing of all the Calm Exercises. Essentially, it is a variation of Calm Exercise Three where the breathing flows just as naturally. You can work your own breathing pattern for this exercise. If you have a large lung capacity (or if you're fit), you can do the whole movement in one breath. Most people will find it easier to do it in two breaths: in and out as the hands rise; in and out as the hands fall. Remember to make the hands/arms movement *as slow and fluid as possible*.

1) *Countenance and stance as specified.*
2) *Bend knees slightly until almost bowlegged. Fingers entwined, arms straight down, palms upward (see figure 4).*
3) *Breathe in and raise cupped hands (as if drawing water from a well) to mouth.*

4) *As hands pass face (rising upwards), turn cupped hands away from you so palms face out (see figure 5) and begin to exhale.*

5) *Rising on your toes, continue hands upwards until* palms face ceiling *and arms are fully extended upwards.*

6) *Breathe in as you reverse the action, bringing hands past face level (see figure 6).*

7) *Exhale as you sink back into the bow-legged position with arms (fingers still entwined) lowered in front of you (see figure 4).*

8) *Repeat exercise at least five times until your breathing is deep and regular.*

9) *Relax.*

Palms
upwards

figures 4, 5 and 6
CALM EXERCISE 4

If you are still restless after performing these Calm Exercises, do the following (while standing or reclining).

1) *Tense one set of muscles (e.g. arms). Then relax (so you know what 'relaxed' feels like).*
2) *Tense another set of muscles (e.g. abdomen).*
3) *Relax them.*
4) *Repeat with neck, back, legs, hands, feet, buttocks, chest.*
5) *Then perform the Calm Exercises.*

CHAPTER 7

Continuous Calm

'Don't meditate; be in meditation.'
Buddha

TO GET THE MOST BENEFITS from the Calm
Technique, it needs some sort of carrythrough into your
everyday life. Being calm and contented for an hour
a day is one thing, but carrying that feeling with you
all day requires more effort. Undoubtedly, the Calm
Technique performed every morning and evening will
give you a more balanced and peaceful perspective, and
a more harmonious outlook than if you didn't use it at
all, but can the Calm Technique by itself maintain that
unique sense of calm throughout each and every day?

Probably not. To realize the full benefits of the
Calm Technique in every moment of your life, it needs

to become part of your life. Not just in the morning and evening, but during your day as well.

THE CALM TECHNIQUE IN ACTION

Not all meditations are performed from a static position. In fact, some very well-known types are extremely active. Yet they all share a common objective with the Calm Technique: their goal is simply 'being'; their method is through centring the attention on just one activity. So whether the path is Zen-inspired archery, the ballet-like movements of Tai Chi, the feverish dancing of the Dervishes, the martial-art styles of China and Japan, or even the famous 'Little Way' of St Teresa of Lisieux, the objective remains the same for all: forgetting the distractions and centring the attention on the task at hand (i.e. living just in that moment).

After you have been performing the Calm Technique for a while, you will begin to find the process of 'hearing' your Calm Expression much easier. You will be able to make it much more a part of your everyday life. In time, you will be able to relax the rules; you will be able to meditate in rooms that are not darkened, that are not even quiet. You will be able to steal calming moments in places when you're surrounded by people and traffic. You'll be able to do it with your eyes open, when you're standing, when you're reclining. (Don't try these things in the early stages as they will only tend to lead you astray.) And even though your quiet, private morning and evening meditations will still be the basis of your Calm Technique practice, you will also be able to apply the 'Calm Technique in Action' throughout your day. It works similarly to the stationary version.

Try it when walking.

You begin by just walking – eyes unfocused (open please), looking in front of you, hands swinging loosely as you walk. Relax your neck, face and arms. After a minute or so, your hands will feel quite limp and heavy – maybe your fingers will tingle slightly. Your breathing will be deep and even, as it is in the Calm Exercises.

Then begin to listen to your footsteps as you walk. Listen to them until they fill your attention. Ignore the traffic sounds, hear only your footstep as each foot touches the ground. Be aware only of your walking. Relax into this one activity until you are totally absorbed by it. Forget the passers-by. You may have to stop at the traffic lights or cross through heavy traffic, but these things you will do safely and instinctively; your peripheral vision will warn you about oncoming cars and 'Don't Walk' signs. Let your awareness be filled with the rhythm of your walking; ignore everything else. That you're on the footpath and cars are going past means nothing: hear only that soothing sound of your own footsteps. Feel only the breath in your lungs and the path beneath your feet. In minutes you will have forgotten the distractions, the traffic jams, the sweaty crowds: you'll be meditating. It will feel a little different from your regular morning and evening meditation, but it can be just as effective.

As an alternative to listening to your footsteps (or your breathing, if you prefer), you could 'hear' your

Calm Expression emanating from your Calm Centre as you do during the Calm Technique. You could also try 'hearing' it when you're bouncing on a trampoline. Or travelling on the train or bus, when you're in the bath or on the beach, when you're waiting in a long queue – you'll find no end of possible places where you can perform the Calm Technique.

You will find that the 'Calm Technique in Action' can be an effortless way of recharging your energies and exorcising your anger and anxieties during a working day. In fact, *to maintain a sense of calm, it is essential that you devote some moments of your working day to the Calm Technique or the Calm Technique in Action*. Even if it's only for three or five minutes.

Effective though they may be, these variations should not replace your morning or evening performances of the Calm Technique. They are not intended as a substitute for those two sessions, more a calm bonus to help you maintain your peace and harmony throughout the day.

THE CALM BREAK

The most stressful environment any of us ever has
to face is the daily grind: the office, the factory, the
building site, even the home. It's almost as if there were
some cynical design to turn our workplaces into little
purgatories of competitiveness and insecurity. Even
when we enjoy every stimulating moment of our
working day, we still have to contend with more stress
situations per minute than in almost any other activity
outside wartime. In surroundings like these, even the
best morning and evening meditations are sometimes
insufficient to compensate.

In these times, even two minutes of the Calm
Technique during your working day will bring significant benefits. Five minutes is better. Instead of a
coffee break (remember coffee fuels tension), take a
Calm Break. A five-minute walk by yourself, hearing
only your Calm Expression or your footsteps, will do
more to help you through the day than all the coffee in

the world. A five-minute meditation in some quiet place will give you more energy and enthusiasm for the rest of the day than any caffeine and sugar break. A Calm Break can make your day.

This is not hiding from reality, it is simply maximizing your potential. If everyone in your workplace is slowly (or quickly) going mad and cultivating stress-related ailments, it is not a 'reality' you should be party to. Besides, you will find that having a sense of order and calm in your work life will not only be more beneficial to you and your work, but it will have a calming influence on all who work with you.

I'll give you an example. A man I met, let's call him Peter, worked in an advertising agency. As you may guess, advertising is one of the most insecure, political and volatile industries one can work in; the stress-related casualty rate is quite staggering. Peter learned a meditation method which was of great benefit to his life in general. But he still had to spend twelve hours a day in an insecure and highly stressful environment. He needed more. When exposed to the principle of taking a Calm Break several times a day in the seclusion of his own mind, away from the pressures and the politics and the decisions, he considered it blatant escapism. He thought it would take away the hard business edge that he'd spent so long developing. He felt sure it would take away his drive, his hunger for success, his aggression. He felt that it would soften him professionally. Eventually his work situation took its toll, and he made the decision to quit the business.

Persuaded to give it one more go, only this time taking Calm Breaks several times throughout the day, he tried again. Usually at this particular stage of these types of stories, the subject gets everything out of life he wants, with no extra effort, and everything changes overnight. We all know that, in real life, such things don't happen. However, Peter did make an effort to change the way he thought about his work. He sought time to himself during his working day to take stock, to recharge his batteries. He applied the Calm Principles (*see page 148*). He took Calm Breaks. And as soon as he learned to relax he was no longer one of the insecure people of that industry. He was free of doubts and insecurities, and not surprisingly, he was free to do his best work ever. Now he is one of the most relaxed, most sought-after (and most highly paid!) advertising consultants in the country.

After you are very familiar with the Calm Technique, it is beneficial if you practise it occasionally with your eyes open, gazing unfocused at some spot in front of you. Although it may feel a little unusual to you at first, it will soon become second nature. Then, when you have mastered the Calm Technique with your eyes open, you'll find that you can steal moments of privacy during the day without drawing attention to yourself. A three- or five-minute application of the Calm Technique in the office, while travelling to work, standing in a queue or waiting for the lift can work wonders.

THE CALM PRINCIPLE

Even if you'd never read about the Calm Technique, you could still achieve a great measure of calm and wellbeing in your day-to-day life by applying a very simple practice called the Calm Principle. Essentially, it makes every act of your day an act of meditation. Everything you do is done in such a way that it enriches your life and makes you a happier, more contented, more successful human being.

The Calm Principle is deceptively simple. All it demands is that each thing you do, you do completely and to the best of your ability. While you're doing that one thing, you ignore distractions and concentrate all your attention on that one moment. If you have a mundane chore to do, you absorb yourself in it totally without seeking 'relief' through conversation or entertaining thoughts. You approach even the most unexciting or most trivial task as if it were the most important thing that had ever happened in your life.

Because at that very moment, it should be!

Life exists only in the present. 'Future' and 'Past' are nothing more than abstract concepts; yet they dominate our lives and are at the root of almost every emotional disorder or discomfort ever experienced. In Western society, concerns for what's passed and what's yet to happen cause more insecurity, anxiety, fear, frustration and tension than any other condition. The Calm Principle helps you to overcome your regrets about the past and your concerns for the future. The way you do this is simply by concentrating your life in the present, by living each moment to its fullest and by devoting all your attention and appreciation to that moment.

In practice, the Calm Principle means you don't plan your evening's entertainment while you're working during the day; you don't eat while you're watching the television; you don't worry about tomorrow's deadlines while you're performing today's tasks; you never try to do two things at once. You concentrate all of your attention on one single task or activity, on one moment at a time – that is the Calm Principle.

It is important to recognize that the Calm Principle is not concerned with subjugation of the normal workings of the mind. The Calm Principle is about directing your efforts in a more efficient and orderly fashion. Concentrating attention on a single activity is an exercise in centring, just like the Calm Technique. It frees the mind of all distractions and brings maximum effectiveness to each task you perform. And when you have centred your attention, you will work more efficiently with an ever-present sense of calm and fulfilment, regardless of how strenuous the activity is.

When you can focus your attention on the present, you will produce your greatest effort for each individual moment. This is the most efficient way of working; it is also the ideal way for human beings to function. You achieve little when you flit from one subject to another every thirty seconds, or when you concern yourself with the past or the future as you perform other actions. (Not thinking about the past and future also has the calming effect of eliminating most of the problems you *think* you face.) You can really only do one thing effectively at one time; trying to do more tends to produce less.

If you pay meticulous attention to your most minor undertakings, giving the best you are capable of at that moment, you'll be surprised at how calming it can be. Attempting to do several things at once creates anxiety, limits your effectiveness and seldom seems to help deadlines much at all.

On the surface, the Calm Principle appears to go against the conservative ideal by which most of us have been raised: that is, living for the present is short-sighted and self- indulgent; preparing for the future is commendable. This is not what's intended by the Calm Principle. Insisting that your attention be fully focused on what you're doing – the present – does not imply that you should ignore planning. *To plan is an activity of the present* – you can devote all of your attention to this one task for a specified time, make your plans, then move on to your next task. If every activity you undertake is accompanied by concerns for what's ahead, you will be living in a state of tension. Whereas, if you make your plans, then apply your full attention to following them, your efforts are fully directed in the present – and this is the most calming and effective way to operate.

Apply the Calm Principle to driving your car, and you'll drive it in the best and most complete way you can. The driving will absorb all of your attention. You shouldn't distract yourself by compiling a shopping list as you drive or listening to talkback radio. Be totally engrossed in your driving, do it completely and to the best of your ability. Concentrated attention will not only make you one of the safest and most conscientious drivers on the road, but one of the most peaceful.

Take a lesson from your children. Watch how the uncomplicated child lives each moment for the pleasure of that moment. Watch how she or he becomes totally absorbed in the colouring-in, or the sweeping of the floor, or the fantasy of the game. Consider how calm she or he is at that moment. Because children have yet to learn how to worry and distract themselves, they apply the Calm Principle naturally. It is only later in life, when they grow older and 'wiser' that they learn to ignore this fundamental behaviour.

You may argue that a child doesn't have the responsibilities and problems which adults are forced to endure. This is so. But adults so often *assume* responsibilities and problems that they have no hope of controlling or solving at that moment. If you spend the next fifteen years worrying about how you're going to afford to enjoy your retirement, you'll have wasted fifteen years and probably soured yourself for retirement anyway. If you must worry about a problem, then set aside a period of time for worrying about that problem. Apply all of your attention to it for a specified period of time, then go on to your next task or activity. If you find you have too much on your plate to be able to devote all of your attention to one task at a time, you have too much on your plate! Simple, isn't it?

You can apply the Calm Principle to everything you do. When you're eating, savour every smell, sight and bite (you'll eat less this way and appreciate it more), be totally aware of even the most subtle colours, tastes and textures; become one with the eating. The same when you're washing the dishes. Or pulling the weeds. Or painting a landscape. Or reading a book. If you want to listen to the radio, turn it on and listen to it completely. Don't listen to it while you're reading. It is a popular misconception that having the radio playing while you drive or work is relaxing. It is distracting. And even though it may take your mind off the task somewhat, it does so at the expense of your sense of calm. It creates restlessness.

Dividing your attention creates tension; centring your attention on only one activity (concentration) is not only calming, but is the most productive way you can function.

CONTINUOUS CALM

These very simple practices can have a profound effect
on your day. They are so easy to include in your daily
routine, and can be performed almost anywhere you go
without drawing attention to yourself. Apply the Calm
Principle and find a few extra minutes during the day
for a Calm Break.

Only then will you learn how to enjoy and
appreciate every aspect of life *as it's happening*. Only
then will you be blessed with a permanent sense of calm
and order.

LIFESTYLE CONSIDERATIONS

As I have said before, the Calm Technique can have a
profound effect on your existence, without asking you
to modify your lifestyle one bit. However, it is only one
aspect of development; it is not the universal remedy to
all life's ills. Just as an exercise programme alone with

no consideration to diet will not produce the most healthy body, so too a meditation programme with no consideration of other lifestyle factors cannot be expected to produce the ultimate calm.

Please bear in mind that I am speaking of *optimum* results here. The Calm Technique works in its own right and needs no dietary or exercise assistance to be a great comfort and benefit in your life. However, if you combine the Calm Technique with other programmes, the results will be even greater.

One of the unique characteristics of the Calm Technique is that after you have been using it for some time, you begin to grow more aware of yourself. You begin to get in touch with the subtleties of your own physiology. Your body will tell you that it doesn't approve of large doses of alcohol, drugs or cigarette smoke. Your body will tell you that certain foods are more acceptable than others. Your body will tell you that you need a certain amount of exercise.

This new awareness of the Self is part of the

reason why those who practise the Calm Technique find it easier to give up smoking, reduce drinking, live without drugs. Obviously the elimination of stress has a lot to do with this. But equally as important is a new discovery of your own body and make-up. You will *feel* when something is good for you, or when something should be avoided. You may argue that you already know that certain things aren't good for you, that your smoker's cough or hangovers are constant physical reminders of what you're doing to yourself. But with the Calm Technique, your body helps you avoid these things by not craving them. To enjoy life to the fullest, to be a *complete* human being, pay attention to the four different aspects of your life:

1) The Calm Technique
2) Diet
3) Exercise
4) Attitude

THE CALM TECHNIQUE

The Calm Technique or some other form of meditation is essential for a well-balanced, happy, healthy way of life.

DIET

If there's one thing that affects your state of mind as much as your health, it's your diet. It is common enough knowledge that diet affects the emotions and mental state as much as it does the body. You really are what you eat.

There is no need for this book to explore diet in great depth, many other publications cover it. Nevertheless, there is one dietary principle which deserves to be highlighted over and above everything else: moderation.

Moderation in diet is a principle that has been ignored by the hundreds of books which come out each year on this subject. The fact is, no-one ever grew rich (or became noticed) by preaching moderation. A scientist or dietician is not going to be considered very innovative nor is she or he going to create any new fad or movement by encouraging moderation. Yet this is the most obvious and most sensible practice to adopt.

We all know that the modern person eats far too much. The average person's calorie consumption far exceeds recommended daily requirements. Today's average food intake is more suited to the requirements of primitive man with his regular episodes of 'fight or flight' than it is to a modern person's hours in the office, in front of a television or driving a cab.

Eat less, unless, you're *already* eating less.

Moderation in choice of food is also becoming a rare principle these days. As every second person you meet seems to be advocating the 'Drinking Girl's Diet' or the 'Banana Diet' or the 'Armed Services Diet' or the 'Hamburger-and-Cola Diet', is it any wonder that the 'Moderate Diet' is vanishing? The 'Moderate Diet' is just what you learned at school: sensible, varied proportions from each of the five food groups.

Eat more fruit and vegetables, especially raw ones.

Choose wholegrain rather than processed. Drink more (unchilled) water than you think you need. Choose herbal teas in preference to tea or coffee (as soon as you stop comparing them with 'real' teas, you'll learn to appreciate the calming and soothing effect they can produce).

Choose foods rich in vitamin A (yoghurt, cream, butter, eggs, liver, carrots, leafy green vegetables, fruit) which counteract the ravages of stress. Choose even more vitamin C foods (fruit and vegetables), which are required in greater proportions as stress levels increase. They also have a positive effect on one's mental health. And, most importantly of all, make your diet rich in vitamin B foods (beans, lentils, peas, nuts, seeds, wheat germ, bran, wholegrains, brewer's yeast, liver, eggs, milk, cheese, yoghurt, meat, fish, poultry and green leafy vegetables). Remember that, like most vitamins, the B vitamins are rapidly destroyed by light, high temperatures, steam, long cooking and long storage.

Obviously there are things to avoid: artificial additives of any kind, excessive sugar, salt and spices.

Coffee and alcohol (especially spirits) should be limited. Refined foods of all types should be banished from your diet.

If you follow those simple principles and apply moderation (both in consumption and choice) to your diet, you will enjoy something that most people over-look in their search for sophisticated solutions to simple dietary needs.

In many schools of meditation, diet plays a much larger role. Any serious student of the traditional schools knows that the higher forms of meditation require more disciplines than an hour a day sitting quietly. Diet is one of those disciplines. Such students are very aware that the food they eat has a definite influence on their state of mind. With some foods the effect can be quite extreme, and with others, barely noticeable. Nevertheless, diet does have an influence on the effectiveness of your meditation. How great an influence is a matter for conjecture, but it does exist.

Note: the following dietary discussion is not an integral part of the Calm Technique.

All foods can be divided into three distinct categories: calm, stimulating and lethargic foods. A serious meditator's diet (particularly from the Indian schools) consists mainly of calm foods, with occasional tastes of stimulating foods. Lethargic foods are avoided altogether. You will note that, perhaps with the exception of onion and garlic, the recommended Yogi's diet is virtually the same as your everyday 'alternative lifestyle' diet.

Calm foods are the pure foods which are central to all yogic diets. They are easily digested, cleansing, provide plenty of energy, and most importantly, encourage a calm state of mind. It is generally accepted that these foods are the most suitable foods for human beings.

Calm foods include:
- all kinds of fruits
- most vegetables (with as little cooking as possible)

- nuts and seeds in their natural state
- beans
- grains
- milk and milk products
- herbs and spices (in moderation)

Stimulating foods are the foods which create activity and unrest in the mind. (Many of the lethargic foods also fit this category.) These foods should be used infrequently.

Stimulating foods are:
- excessive spices
- vinegar
- coffee, tea, cola
- all foods with preservatives
- most canned and packaged foods

Lethargic foods are the foods to be avoided. They demand far too much energy and time to digest and create great feelings of inertia. Many of them also fall into the previous category of stimulating foods. Meat for example, being considered in both categories, causes feelings of lethargy, tiredness as well as a general feeling of restlessness.

Lethargic foods do the mind no good whatsoever. They include:

- meat and poultry
- seafood
- refined foods (e.g. white sugar, bread, flour)
- alcohol
- fermented (e.g. pickled) or stale foods

I have omitted some foods from all categories. They are eggs, onions, garlic, chives and leeks. In Raja Yoga's book *Eating for Immortality*, they are classified as lethargic foods to be avoided entirely. However, other books occasionally classify them differently. I am reluctant to cast the deciding vote, so you decide if they are suitable for your diet.

Should you decide that a diet of calm foods (with

moderate amounts of stimulating foods) is for you, consider buying one of the many vegetarian cookbooks which are available. Don't consider this small chapter as the final word on what you can or cannot eat. It is a guide; you would need to study the subject further. If you do decide to pursue such a diet, it is more desirable to change gradually by substituting foods from your present diet with foods from this one. Sudden and radical changes are counterproductive and should be avoided.

EXERCISE

Exercise has to be the most written-about subject of the decade. I wish I could tell you the Calm Technique removes the necessity for exercise (for my own sake as much as yours); however, this is not so.

If the thought of all that sweating and heavy breathing bothers you, forget the gyms and aerobic dancing, and concentrate on long walks. Walking is excellent exercise; it's sensible, effective and requires no special equipment. But the good thing about walking is that you can perform the Calm Technique (*see the 'Calm Technique in Action', page 140*) as you exercise. Then it can be relaxing as well as health-promoting.

Exercise does have an impact on the way you meditate. Any improvement in your general sense of health and wellbeing definitely enhances your performance of the Calm Technique. As well, being able to breathe correctly does wonders for your feelings of calm. When you learn to use the full capacity of your lungs, when you know how to breathe deeply and fully without effort, you will experience a sense of wellbeing similar to that felt by highly conditioned athletes. Read the Calm Exercises (*see page 124*) again, and learn to breathe deeply.

ATTITUDE

Attitude is every bit as important to your overall wellbeing as diet and exercise. A bitter, negative outlook will have a negative effect on your health and happiness. An optimistic, enthusiastic attitude enhances them.

After the Calm Technique, optimism should be your most important behavioural consideration. A positive attitude in your life will bring increased happiness, better health, more effective relationships and improved communications.

For some, optimism is a natural gift. But most of us have to work at it. Still, it's worthwhile! A positive attitude affects every moment of your day, and every person and situation you come in contact with. It's contagious. It's energizing. It's uplifting. It's health-giving. And success in almost every endeavour depends upon it.

There is no secret formula for developing a positive outlook. You simply have to be aware that such an attitude is desirable (that's positive in itself), and go after it with determination. Learn to recognize negative thoughts and feelings so you can replace them with the positive. While this may sound glib and over-simplified, it is the easiest and most successful way of developing optimism. Because a positive frame of mind is so much more powerful than a negative one; negative thoughts and emotions cannot long survive a positive effort to change them.

The Calm Technique is a great vehicle to instil positivity in your day. Begin your day as early as you possibly can with fifteen to thirty minutes of the Calm Technique. On completion, sit in that relaxed state for a few minutes and tell yourself how you're going to vibrate with positive energy all through the day. Picture yourself going through the day with a smile and boundless enthusiasm. Picture yourself looking only for the good in people you come in contact with. You will be amazed at how great an effect these couple of minutes can have on your day.

It may sound obvious, but as well as having the correct attitude, you need to maintain some sort of interest in your life. That means you need to be interested in your occupation as well as your leisure.

You might think it easier for those in the glamour professions to maintain interest in their work than it is for the labourer, or the housewife, or the unemployed. It may well be. Nevertheless, you owe it to yourself to be interested in what you do. If you have the most boring task in the whole world to perform, then be interested in the way *you* perform it. So, while the task may be boring, your performance can be interesting, especially if each thing you do, you do completely. You concentrate only on the task at hand, and let nothing distract you.

As far as your leisure time is concerned. I'm sure you don't need me to tell you how to maintain interest and variety there.

Finally, laugh more. Laughter is unequalled as a therapeutic act. It relaxes all muscles, tensions and anger. Learn to see the funny side of life and your problems will vanish accordingly. Recognize the humorous side of your own personality and actions and you cannot be self-centred (bear in mind that 'self-centred' is completely different from 'centering, to come in contact with self'). Laugh more and you'll stop taking yourself and your life so seriously.

The Calm Technique will have a positive effect on your attitude. The Calm Principle can add interest to your daily routine. Work on your attitude; laugh more; be interested in what you do; maintain a moderate diet and a sensible exercise programme; use the Calm Technique every day and you will get everything you want out of life: peace, health and happiness. No other way can ever compare.

SECTION III

CHAPTER 8

Questions and Answers

'What we need is an enthusiastic but calm state of mind and intense but orderly work.'
Mao Tse-Tung

Following are some of the most commonly asked questions relating to the Calm Technique. If, at the end of this book, you have questions of your own, please feel free to write to Paul Wilson's calm research group, at The Calm Centre, PO Box 404, Northbridge, NSW 2063, Australia. Or log on to, http://www.calmcentre. com. You can also e-mail the author at, paulwil@calm centre.com.au.

Q: *There are many different types of meditation. Which type is superior?*

A: It is a dangerous precedent for a self-improvement book to admit that there might be more than one 'right' direction to follow. However, the truth is there are *thousands* of 'right' directions. The fact that you meditate is all that's important. How you meditate is a matter of personal preference. The important thing is that you choose one type of meditation and practise it sincerely and consistently. As far as the quality of the technique itself is concerned, Zen meditation is no better than Tai Chi; Raja Yoga is no better than reciting the Rosary; Sufi rugweaving is no better than Dervish whirling. As long as each of them is practised sincerely and *consistently*, each is as effective as the other. The only advantage the Calm Technique has over all of them is that it's so easy to learn. In my humble opinion, that is a real superiority.

Q: *How important is Indian meditation to the Calm Technique?*

A: I have never seen a hint of evidence which shows that culturally based formulae have any special spiritual relevance when they are exported. No doubt, because of some very old traditions, there is a popular misconception that India has some sort of franchise over proper meditation practices. Experience and common sense have shown that this is not so. Most Western teachers these days tend to agree that you must approach your particular meditation programme from within the framework of your own culture and environment. While this is not intended to denigrate the imported varieties (many of which have a great deal to offer), there has been too much of an Eastern bias in meditation. The Calm Technique is for everyone.

Q: *Is it possible to produce an experience similar to the Calm Technique by using drugs?*

A: Drugs will never equal the purity of the Calm Technique experience. The ability to focus your attention on one thing is sometimes possible under the effects of marijuana, but the experience is shallow and meaningless. Focusing in itself is not meditation, especially when it is enhanced by a *stimulant* such as marijuana is. You can achieve this same capacity to focus through your own efforts with the Calm Technique. With the Calm Technique you do it with a highly alert, perfectly balanced frame of mind. There is no comparison.

Q: *Does the Calm Technique impinge on my religious beliefs?*

A: The Calm Technique offers no spiritual or philo- sophical advice. It is simply a technique for getting the most out of the temporal side of your life. It has no direct relevance at all to your religious beliefs or lack thereof.

Q: *Would you call the Calm Technique a trance?*

A: Of a fashion.

Q: *Is it possible that the Calm Technique could be a form of self-hypnosis?*

A: Hypnosis, being a state where you place your will in the hands of a third party, is the opposite to the Calm Technique. Hypnosis, as a means of limiting the consciousness, differs from the Calm Technique, which is a means of expanding the consciousness. The physiological state of hypnosis reflects whatever state has been suggested to the subject, while the Calm State is one of wakefulness combined with the calming qualities of deep sleep – a physiological condition that cannot be induced through hypnotism. Hypnotism is usually conducted with a definite goal in mind. The Calm Technique, in itself, has no goal.

Two similarities do exist, however. First, hypnosis and the Calm Technique both depend on highly focused attention. Second, hypnosis and the Calm Technique are both self-induced states. While self-induction may not appear to sit comfortably with the definition of hypnosis (a state where one's consciousness and will are placed under the control of a third party), it is the only way the hypnotic state can be attained. Having said that, self-hypnosis induces a physiological state that is similar, or even the same as meditation. I suppose you could even say that most forms of meditation are essentially self-hypnosis.

However, the most significant difference between the two states is simply their reasons for being. Hypnotism is concerned with *instilling* 'truths' and attitudes in a subject's subconscious, whereas the Calm Technique is dedicated to *discovering* the truth that already exists there. Which means there can be no comparison.

Q: What if the phone rings in the middle of the Calm Technique?

A: Answer it. Before you begin the Calm Technique, you should always ensure there is nothing to disturb you. It's most annoying. However, should you overlook taking the phone off the hook or something like that, an unanswered telephone will do a lot more to upset your equilibrium than getting up and answering it.

Q: What do I do about an itch or a cramp during the Calm Technique?

A: You have two choices. Ignore it and maintain your attention only on your Calm Expression, or scratch. You will find that minor itches and discomforts grow in intensity the more you think about them. Usually, they are just tricks of the mind intended to distract you from your task. Don't get obsessed about ignoring them, but ignore them if you can.

Q: *What is the ideal time of day for the Calm Technique?*

A: Always as early as possible in the morning, preferably in the peace and calm before the world wakes and goes about its business. As soon as you are washed and awake, begin the Calm Technique. You'll find that rising half an hour earlier than you normally would will still leave you feeling rested.

Q: *What is the ideal length of time for the Calm Technique?*

A: This is best decided through experience. In the beginning, fifteen to twenty minutes is the recommended time. If you don't have fifteen minutes, make it ten. A short session is better than none at all.

Q: *How can you tell when the twenty minutes are up?*

A: Use a clock (careful of the alarm) and take a peek occasionally. Better still though, is to trust your intuition. Your body clock works most accurately of all.

Q: Does it matter if you go longer?

A: In the early stages, it is best not to continue the Calm Technique for more than about thirty minutes. As you become more familiar with it, then certainly extend your meditations as you feel necessary.

Q: What if you get tired, or go to sleep?

A: If you feel sleepy, try the Calm Technique with your eyes partially opened. If you do happen to doze off, you'll usually wake within a short time. It's not as if you'll sleep all day and miss a day's work.

Q: How do you know if it's been a good meditation?

A: The fact that you did it makes it a good meditation. However, there will almost certainly be times when nothing much will happen and you'll go through a rather dull period. These are the times when you must persist (remember the exercise analogy) because the rewards are greater for those who persevere. Sometimes, usually after a dull stretch, things get even better than they were before it.

Q: *I've been told that some people just aren't the type who can meditate. What sort of people are these?*

A: Lazy people. Or people who haven't read *The Calm Technique*.

Q: *How old do you have to be to start using the Calm Technique?*

A: While there is no age limit for using the Calm Technique at all, common sense says that it should be reserved for those who are old enough to appreciate what it can mean. It is possible to teach certain forms of meditation (even the Calm Technique) to small children. But why?

Q: *Is it possible for several people to do the Calm Technique together?*

A: A group meditation encourages a wonderfully peaceful environment which is one of the rare pleasures of life. Even though the Calm Technique is a personal and solitary event, performing it in the company of others creates a group dynamic which has to be experienced to be believed. Do it whenever you can.

Q: *Surely stress has a place within one's physiology?*

A: It certainly does. Not only are certain amounts of stress and tension quite normal in daily life, but they're essential to the performance of many natural functions. Imagine running in the Olympics without any pre-race anxiety. Would you feel comfortable with a general who felt totally at ease about the battle he was just about to commit you to? We all feel safer when air traffic controllers work with a *moderate* level of stress. And should you ever be confronted with a real 'fight or flight' situation, you will be only too pleased for that stress.

But what concerns us and the Calm Technique is accumulated and unrelieved stress. Stress that is ever present, that feeds on itself, that depresses and debilitates. Whether it is obvious or not, it is a fact of life that the majority of Western people suffer from stress-related conditions and disorders. The Calm Technique is a major step towards relief.

Q: *What about in those times of great stress when you have real problems?*

A: Those times of great personal problems and stress are the times when you need the Calm Technique most of all. Unfortunately, they are usually the most difficult occasions to practise it. You have things on your mind, things you have to do, things that distract you. Nevertheless, these are the times when you have to persist. Do the Calm Exercises. Devote a bit more time to each Calm Technique session. I usually find it takes me about fifteen minutes just to start meditating on such occasions, so perhaps you have to dedicate more than thirty minutes to the full exercise, maybe up to forty-five minutes or an hour.

Q: *Sometimes I just fidget for twenty minutes and it doesn't seem to work at all. Am I doing something wrong?*

A: Try the Calm Exercises first, which should make a difference. If not, perhaps you're just going through a dry period in which case you should persist. However, if things seem really difficult, be content to sit for twenty minutes and enjoy the solitude. And if things get really desperate on any occasion, postpone till the next session.

Q: *Sometimes after twenty minutes I realize that I don't remember a single moment of that time; it's just as if I closed my eyes one instant, and opened them the next, with twenty minutes missing in between. Is this desirable?*

A: It happens sometimes. I'm not sure why. All I
     know is it is pleasant, but it is not something you
     should pursue as an objective, and is one of those
     things that happen in meditation.

Q: *I find it almost impossible to fit two twenty-minute
     sessions into my schedule. What should I do?*
A: It would be glib of me to say 'rearrange your sched-
     ule'. But it does work. You'll never regret rising a
     half hour earlier (except when the alarm sounds) to
     perform the Calm Technique. If you can't manage it
     twice a day, then at least do it once a day. Then when
     you are very familiar with the technique, you can
     grab moments here and there throughout your day.
     Ensure you do it once a day though.

Q: *What if I miss a few days?*
A: Missing a few days is undesirable but shouldn't
     mean the end of your programme. Resume it as
     soon as you can.

Q: *What if there's nowhere I can do it?*

A: This sometimes happens when you live in a crowded house or you're staying with people you don't know too well. On such occasions you can rise early, you can take walks in the park (wonderful for the Calm Technique), do it on the train, in fact, you can do it practically anywhere (and it doesn't frighten the horses).

Q: *Why do you say the Calm Technique should be done before meals?*

A: Two reasons. The first is because the metabolism slows down and your digestive process is suspended during the Calm Technique. If you have just finished eating that's not a very healthy situation to be in. The second reason is because the sounds and discomforts of delayed digestion are quite a distraction during the Calm Technique. Do it before meals or more than two hours after.

Q: *I've been told that meditation is a great time for problem-solving. Is there some way I can use the Calm Technique for any practical purposes?*

A: The Calm Technique is a time for 'hearing' your Calm Expression, not for solving problems. Nevertheless, it is an excellent prelude to a time of problem solving. In those peaceful moments when you have *finished* the Calm Technique, your mind is fresh, creative and alert. It is an excellent time for problem-solving and creative thinking. Use those moments well.

Q: *And what about the ideas that come into your mind while you're doing the Calm Technique – should they be acted upon?*

A: You'll find that your distractions will become more and more inventive during the Calm Technique. Some of the schemes and concepts that you'll think of (when you're supposed to be thinking only of your Calm Expression) will seem quite extraordinary. As a general rule, these schemes and concepts should be treated like any other distraction that crosses your mind: you should forget them and go back to your Calm Expression.

Q: *Is it possible to change your Calm Expression after you have been using it for a while?*

A: Your Calm Expression is a very special part of your meditation development. It should remain an important part of your life and, once accepted, never changed. If at any stage you decide to further your meditation studies with another teacher, that teacher may wish to give you another mantra. In such a case, you will already have decided to search further than the Calm Technique so you will feel no compunction about changing your Calm Expression (nor should you, because in such a situation, change is perfectly acceptable). I can foresee no reasons other than the one just mentioned for wanting to change it. After all, the Calm

Expression is meant to be a meaningless word or phrase. However, if you feel really strongly about it, change. But try to select a suitable one in the first place.

Q: *Some places say you should never tell anyone your mantra. What happens if you do?*

A: It is best not to discuss your Calm Expression or mantra (unless it is with a teacher of meditation). Some schools of thought forbid the mention of the word ever again. I believe it is better left undiscussed. Your Calm Expression is something very private, something which is only ever heard in the inner recesses of your mind. To treat it as an ordinary word or as a conversation topic is to lessen its importance in your mind. Better to leave it alone.

Q: *Sometimes I'm troubled by quite hateful thoughts while I'm meditating? How can I stop them?*

A: Whatever the content of these thoughts, they are nothing but distractions. Go back to your mantra and forget them.

Q: *I've heard that some people go astral travelling and have visions while they're meditating. Is this true?*

A: In all schools of meditation, from the East and the West, the attitude towards paranormal happenings is the same: ignore them. They may be interesting, you may even think them relevant, but they have nothing to do with your meditation and should be ignored. If such an event should present itself to you (and that would be extremely rare), give it no more thought than you would to an itch or a fantasy. It is only your mind trying to distract you from your purpose, which is your Calm Expression.

Q: *What about levitation?*

A: Has nothing to do with the Calm Technique.

Q: *Can the Calm Technique cure insomnia?*

A: Much insomnia is caused by tension and stress. If you can remove the stress and tension, it follows that you'll sleep better. People who use the Calm Technique do sleep more restfully than they did before they practised it. (This is based entirely on subjective reports, I have seen no in-depth studies on the subject.) Those whose insomnia was a product of stress definitely find relief in the Calm Technique. However, whether the Calm Technique can help *all* insomniacs, I am unsure.

Q: *Can the Calm Technique help migraine headaches?*

A: As above.

Q: *Can the Calm Technique help me give up smoking?*

A: Because the Calm Technique is a discipline designed to contain the will and master the senses, it is a great support to anyone contemplating a smoking cure, or a drinking cure, or any sort of cure at all. It does this in three ways. The first is when it strengthens the will. This happens with time. The second occurs when you grow more aware of your body and know what is good or harmful for it. Your body will then encourage you to give up smoking (or whatever). The third reason is simply that you will be more calm and relaxed after a time with the Calm Technique and this provides the greatest assistance of all to giving up. (Assuming of course that you accept the popular theory that smoking is just another symptom of stress.)

If you practise the Calm Technique and follow the five suggestions outlined, I promise you'll be able to give up smoking more easily than you would ever have thought possible. (The same applies for drink and drug problems.)

FIVE WAYS TO OVERCOME ADDICTION
1) Practise the Calm Technique regularly.
2) Instead of *giving up* smoking (drinking or

whatever), *take up* non-smoking. Take up feeling healthy. Take up being able to breathe properly, being able to taste food again. Take up being socially acceptable. Take up being good to be around. The correct attitude is essential. Don't believe any of those clichés about 'getting bad-tempered' or 'getting fat' or 'suffering from nerves'; these are all little tricks to delude yourself into going back to smoking. If you adopt and believe in the positive approach of 'taking up non-smoking', you won't suffer any of those negative reactions.

3) Begin a new exercise programme and diet (assuming you have room for improvement) at the same time. You'll find that when the benefits of one begin to fade, the benefits of the other will become obvious. You'll be encouraged to continue because you'll be feeling so good. And you will be feeling good!

4) Plan the day you're taking up non-smoking (or

whatever) a week in advance. Mark it prominently on your calendar. Refer to it every day leading up to the event. Remember it well after you have taken the plunge. It will be a very important day in your life.

5) Never touch another cigarette (or whatever). There is no such thing as a light smoker (or drinker or drug user). There are only those who pause before taking it up heavily again. Your mind will play many tricks to persuade you that you can have just one smoke every now and then. *But you can't*. When you take up non-smoking, take it up forever.

Q: You mean the Calm Technique increases willpower?
A: Definitely.

Q: Will I ever reach the stage when I don't have to meditate any more?
A: No. But after you've been meditating for some

time, you won't want to stop. You will look forward to and enjoy it for its own sake. The time will come though, when you'll be able to reach the Calm State with very little effort. You will almost be able to reach that state at will. But that's something you have to look forward to.

CHAPTER 9

How to Stay Calm

*'When a man can still his senses
I call him illuminated.'*
Sri Krsna

NOW YOU SHOULD BE READY to apply the Calm
Technique. In the early stages, your greatest obstacle is
simply expecting too much. I know you've read a whole
book on the subject, but the Calm Technique is subtle
and far from 'exciting' as far as experiences go. Don't
expect to be riveted by your Calm Expression from the
beginning. It will probably be several years before you
will be able to spend a full twenty minutes with nothing
but the Calm Expression in your consciousness. The
reason why the Calm Technique is such a successful
builder of character and appreciation is a direct result

of your *not* being able to maintain your Calm Expression for extended periods in your consciousness. The struggle is what's important, not the result. The Calm Technique will be a success if you work hard and conscientiously at it, not just because you become proficient at it.

I urge you to persist with it for at least a couple of months. After that time, I feel absolutely confident you will be as excited about its potential as I am. The biggest hurdle students usually face is after nine to twelve months. This is the time when you begin to grow blasé about what it's doing for you; the improvements aren't as obvious as they were in the beginning. If you let the Calm Technique lapse around this time, it will probably be a few weeks, or even months, before you fully appreciate what you have given up. Then you'll have to start all over again.

That is why it is so important that you learn to appreciate the Calm Technique as something to enjoy in its own right. Learn to appreciate it for what it is rather than what it can do for you. Treasure each time you do it purely for the joy of 'being'. See it as a rare moment of peace and harmony in your day.

In time, the Calm Technique will teach you to recognize your own Calm Centre – that place within you where you will always find a few moments of true peace, regardless of what's going on around you. When you are familiar with your Calm Centre, you will always have a base, you will cease to have regrets about the past and concerns for the future, you will know the joy of living each moment to the fullest.

When you have been meditating for some time, new directions will reveal themselves to you. I have no idea what they might turn out to be, but you can investigate them in the knowledge that your intuition, your real self, will be more at the fore than it has ever been before.

I have cautioned you about intellectual and spiritual promiscuity. Changing from technique to technique, or guru to guru, is just another way of distracting yourself and diverting your attention from its real path. Certainly feel free to broaden your knowledge and appreciation as far as it is possible. But endeavour to build on each experience rather than to seek new ones each time you grow bored. The Calm Technique is an ideal base on which to build.

Use the Calm Technique faithfully and it will be a positive influence in your life. Embrace it and you will have increased health, happiness and harmony in everything you do. Depend on it and you will enjoy a true sense of calm in this troubled old world.